Farm Animals

Dot-to-Dot

Connect
the Dots &
Color

Evan & Lael Kimble

Sterling Publishing Co., Inc.
New York

This book is for all the animals who have become friends to people,
and for all the people who have become friends to animals.

10 9 8 7 6 5 4 3 2 1

Published by Sterling Publishing Co., Inc.
387 Park Avenue South, New York, NY 10016
© 2004 by Evan and Lael Kimble
Distributed in Canada by Sterling Publishing
c/o Canadian Manda Group, One Atlantic Avenue, Suite 105
Toronto, Ontario, Canada M6K 3E7
Distributed in Great Britain and Europe by Chris Lloyd at Orca Book
Services, Stanley House, Fleets Lane, Poole BH15 3AJ, England
Distributed in Australia by Capricorn Link (Australia) Pty. Ltd.
P.O. Box 704, Windsor, NSW 2756, Australia

Sterling ISBN 1-4027-0993-5

CONTENTS

ALLIGATOR

TYPE OF ANIMAL: Reptile

WILD OR DOMESTICATED: Wild

JOB ON THE FARM: One kind of alligator farm is a place where alligators are nursed back to health if they have been injured. When they are well, they are returned to the wild. The other kind of farm is one that raises alligators for their hides and their meat.

DIFFERENT KINDS: There are two basic types of alligator. The American alligator, found only in the southeastern United States, is quite large; the Chinese alligator is much smaller.

WHAT IT EATS: Smaller alligators eat snails, frogs, insects, and little fish. Larger ones eat fish, turtles, snakes, waterfowl, small mammals, and smaller alligators.

HOW FARMERS CARE FOR IT: Alligators are kept in an outside pen with a small pond or pool. They need the temperature to be in the mid-80s (29°C). Some are kept inside in order for them to keep warm. They are fed small animals, fish, and alligator chow.

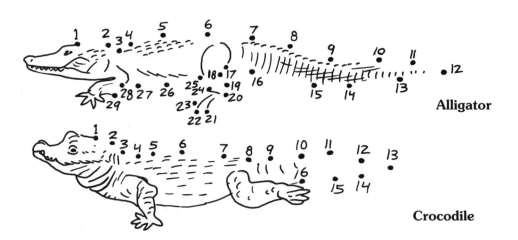

Alligator

Crocodile

Crocodiles are very similar to alligators, but they are larger, don't have an overbite, and are found in more parts of the world.

ALPACA

TYPE OF ANIMAL: Mammal

WILD OR DOMESTICATED: Domesticated

JOB ON THE FARM: Alpacas are domesticated members of the camel family, as are llamas. Their job is to give their wool to make clothing. Sometimes they are shown at fairs. For herders in the Andes Mountains of South America, they are an important source of fiber and meat.

DIFFERENT KINDS: There are two different alpaca types, the suri and the huacaya. The suri has fleece that grows long and is silky. The huacaya has a shorter, more dense fleece. Alpaca fibers come in 22 colors. The alpaca's fleece is soft and warm.

WHAT IT EATS: Grass and hay. They are also usually given a mineral supplement.

HOW FARMERS CARE FOR IT: The alpaca is small enough to be handled easily by most people, being only 36" (1m) high at the withers (shoulder). It needs land to graze on, some protection, and toe and dental care.

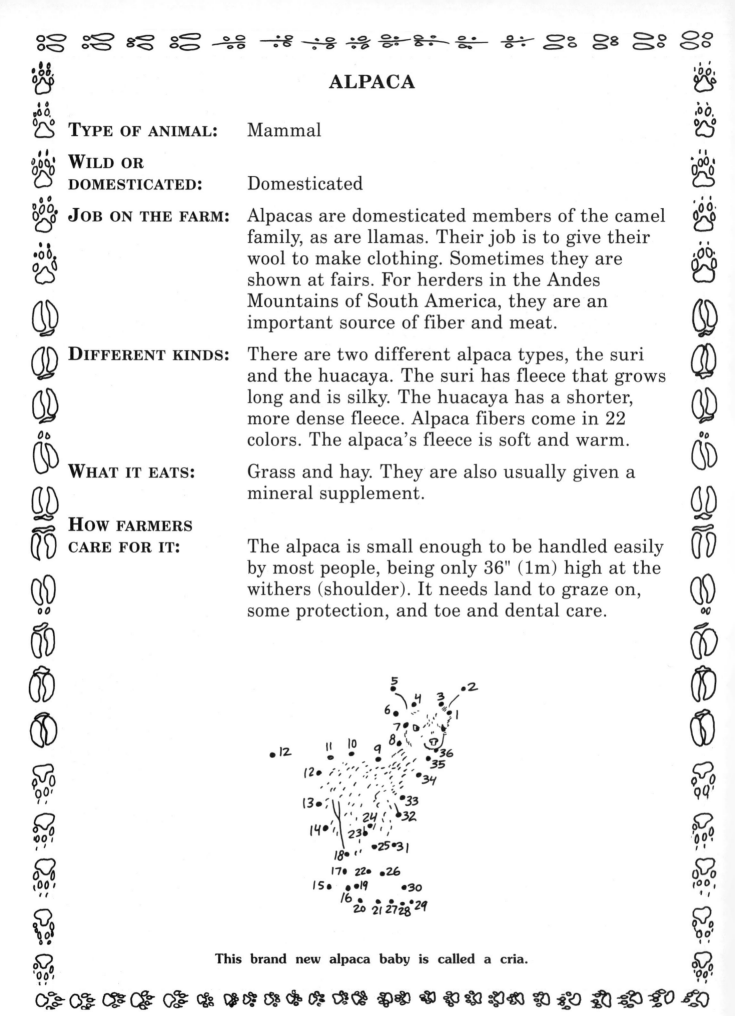

This brand new alpaca baby is called a cria.

BAT

TYPE OF ANIMAL: Mammal

WILD OR DOMESTICATED: Wild

JOB ON THE FARM: Bats are not kept on a farm, but they are usually encouraged to live in the attics of barns or in bat houses that farmers put up in the trees. Bats eat insects, and farmers who have mosquito problems often seek help from bats.

DIFFERENT KINDS: There are nearly 1,000 different kinds of bat in the world.

WHAT IT EATS: Some bats eat fruit, others nectar. There are also meat-eating bats and fish-eating bats. Most bats—seventy percent of them—eat insects. The Little Brown Bat can eat up to 1,200 night-flying insects in one hour!

HOW FARMERS CARE FOR IT: Bat houses are put up 12 to 20 feet (3.6 to 6m) above the ground and near a water source, usually in full sun so they stay warm. If they are put on poles, the bats are safer from predators.

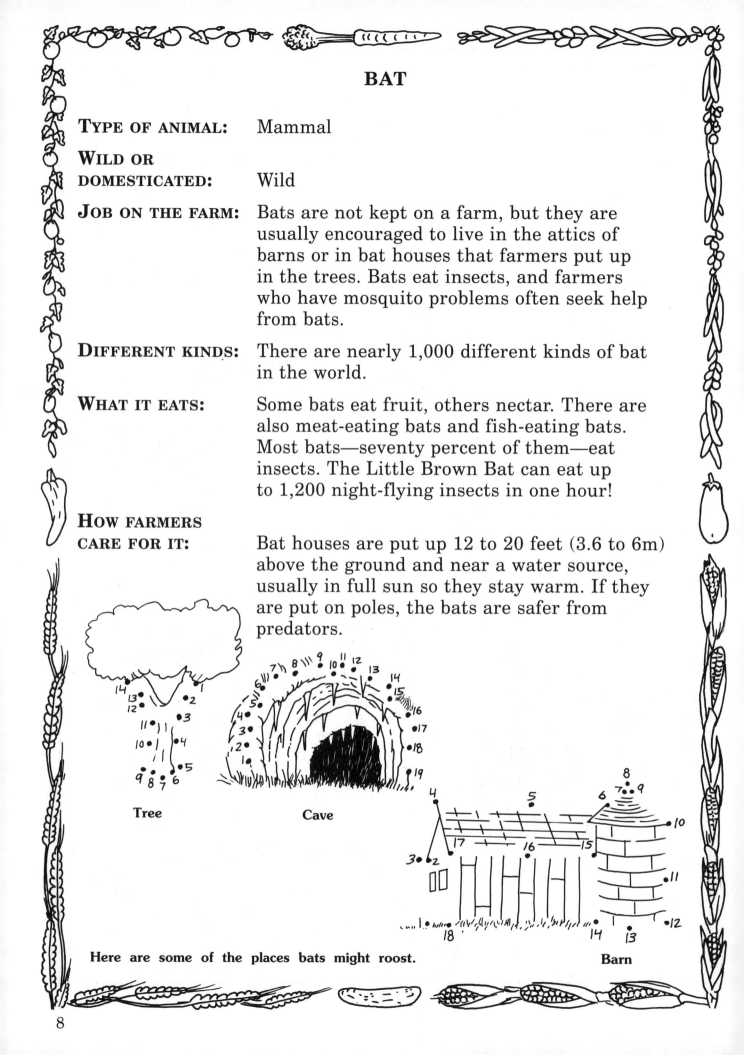

Tree

Cave

Barn

Here are some of the places bats might roost.

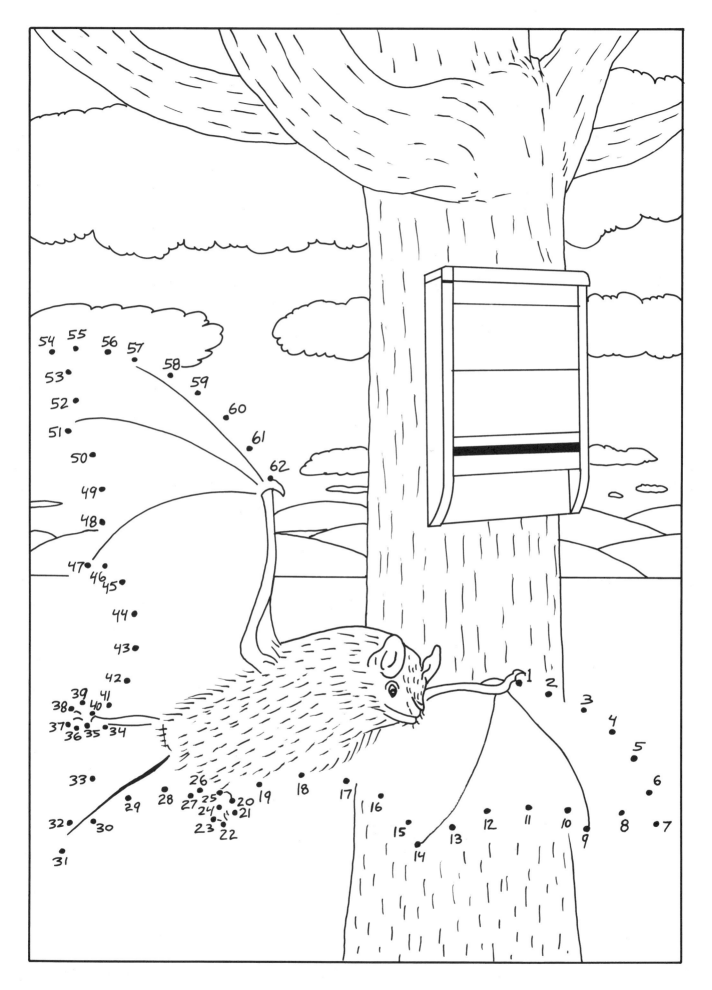

9

BEE

TYPE OF ANIMAL: Insect

WILD OR DOMESTIC: Domesticated

JOB ON THE FARM: To make honey, enough for the hive and extra for the farm. In a hive, as many as 50,000 or more bees live together and work at their own special jobs.

DIFFERENT KINDS: There are approximately 3,500 species of bee. Some bees build their own nests and provide food for only their own offspring. Bumblebees and honey bees live in large groups and do different jobs, bringing back nectar, making wax, feeding babies (nurse bees) and laying eggs (queen bees). Male bees (drones) have only one task, to mate with the queen.

WHAT IT EATS: Bees eat many different foods like fruits, vegetables, and other plants. They eat things that are sweet or bitter—they might like some of your hot dog, for example. And they definitely do eat honey.

HOW FARMERS CARE FOR IT: Beekeepers build hives for the bees to live in. Sometimes they grow certain flowers nearby, because this affects the flavor of the honey. They also collect the honey. When they do this, they wear special suits to keep from getting stung.

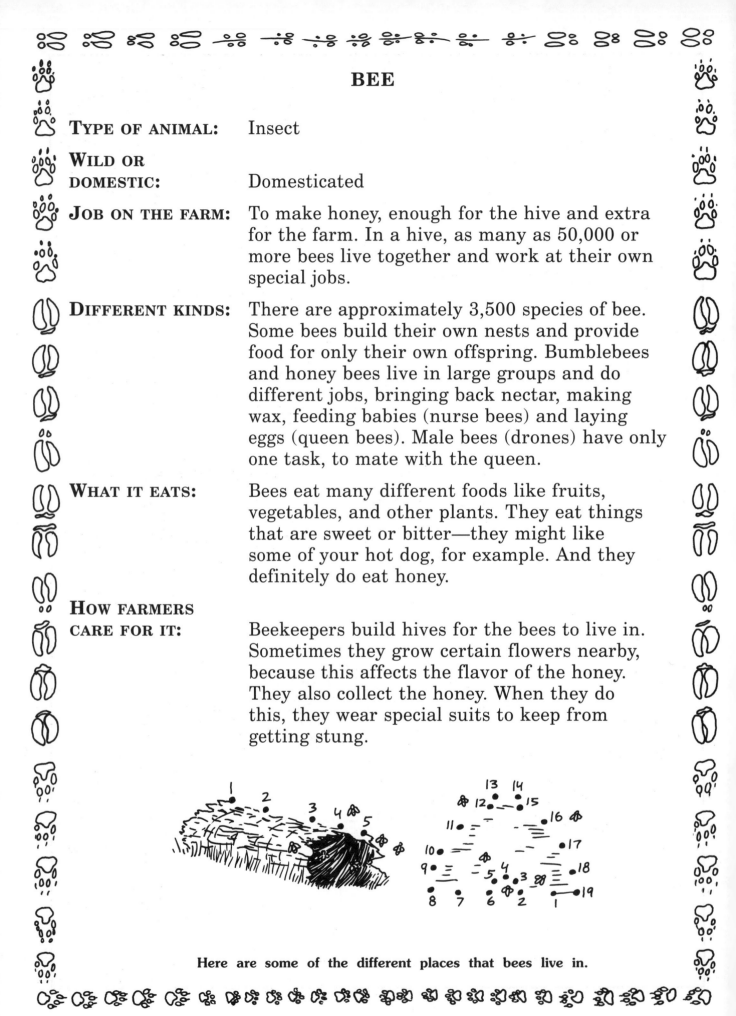

Here are some of the different places that bees live in.

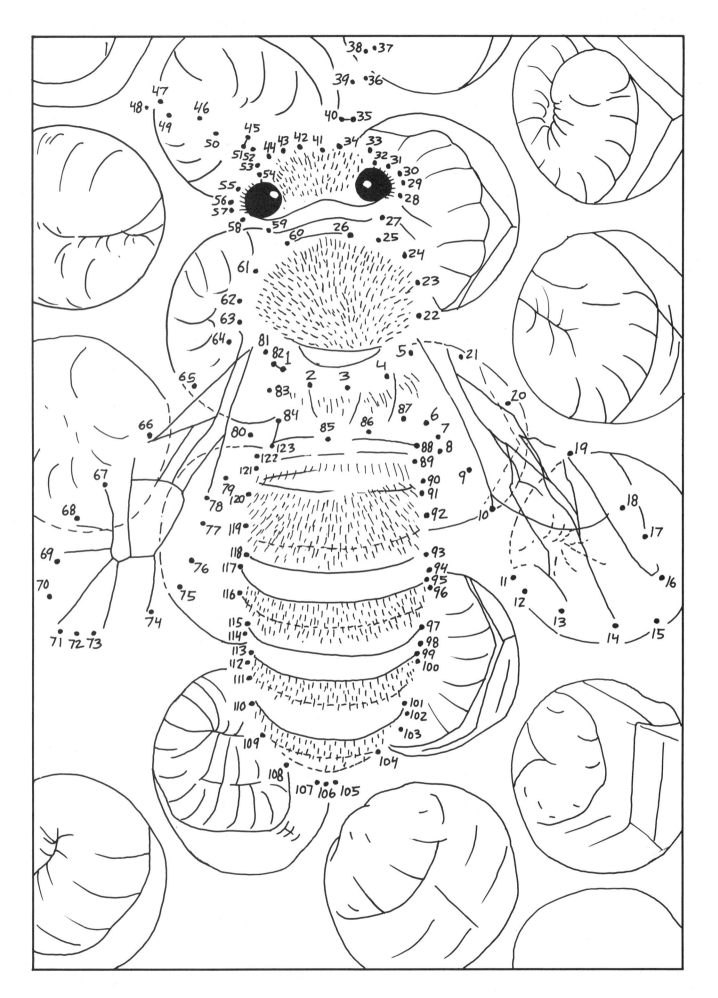

11

BULL

TYPE OF ANIMAL: Mammal

WILD OR DOMESTICATED: Domesticated

JOB ON THE FARM: To help make baby cows or calves. They are kept for breeding and for meat.

DIFFERENT KINDS: There are 270 breeds of cattle. The females are called cows, and the males are called bulls. The most typical breeds you would find on a farm are Ayrshire, Brown Swiss, Guernsey, Holstein, Jersey, and Milking Shorthorn.

WHAT IT EATS: Grass and rough plants. In the winter, they eat hay, corn, barley, grass, and cottonseed in the barn. They also eat cereal, and drink 5 gallons U.S. (4.16 gallons U.K.) of water a day.

HOW FARMERS CARE FOR IT: Farmers keep bulls fenced or penned in, and make sure the area is clean. They provide food and water, especially in winter when there's less to be had.

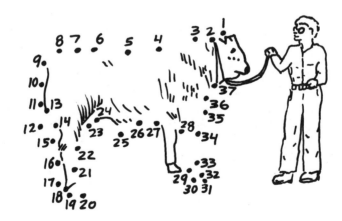

The Chianina is the largest cow or bull. This bull weighs 3,000 pounds (1,361kg) and is 5 feet (1.5m) tall at the top of his shoulder.

CAT

TYPE OF ANIMAL:	Mammal
WILD OR DOMESTICATED:	Domesticated
JOB ON THE FARM:	To catch rats and mice, and keep them out of homes, barns, and other buildings.
DIFFERENT KINDS:	There are many different breeds of cat, at least a hundred, and they are different colors and shapes. Some don't even have a tail. Their hair can be long or short, and their coloring can be solid or mixed, making each one unique.
WHAT IT EATS:	Cats are carnivores, which means they eat meat. Cat food, either dry or a combination of dry and wet, is given. They also enjoy fish, milk, eggs, and cheese.
HOW FARMERS CARE FOR IT:	They feed the cat, give it a home in their house or in another building, and sometimes brush its fur and its teeth.

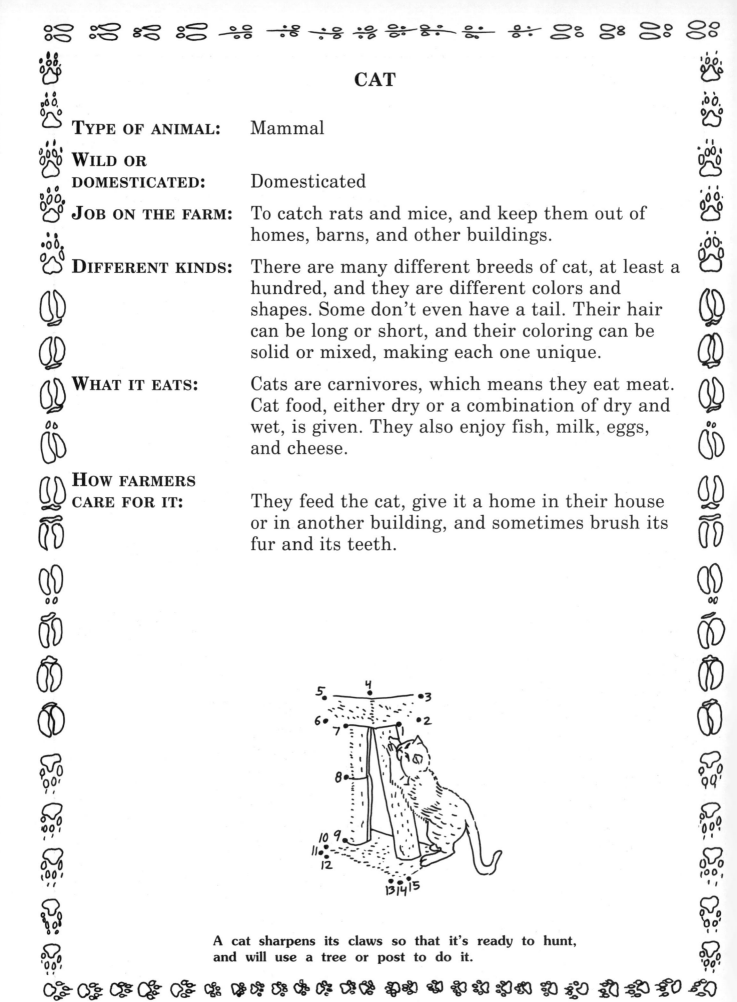

A cat sharpens its claws so that it's ready to hunt, and will use a tree or post to do it.

COW

TYPE OF ANIMAL:	Mammal
WILD OR DOMESTICATED:	Domesticated
JOB ON THE FARM:	Gives milk, which is made into butter, cream, and cheese. Sometimes the cow is raised for its meat. It can also be used for work.
DIFFERENT KINDS:	In the U.S., the most popular cows are Holsteins, because they make lots of milk. Cows produce about 5 gallons U.S. (4.16 gallons U.K.) of milk a day.
WHAT IT EATS:	Grass, hay, and grains. They also like fruit and vegetables. Cows eat cabbage, potatoes, apples, rutabagas, beets, turnips, carrots, broccoli, pumpkins, and squash.
HOW FARMERS CARE FOR IT:	Farmers grow and make hay for the cow to eat. They feed and milk it twice a day. They make sure the cow is healthy. In winter they provide shelter and keep it clean, raking it out often.

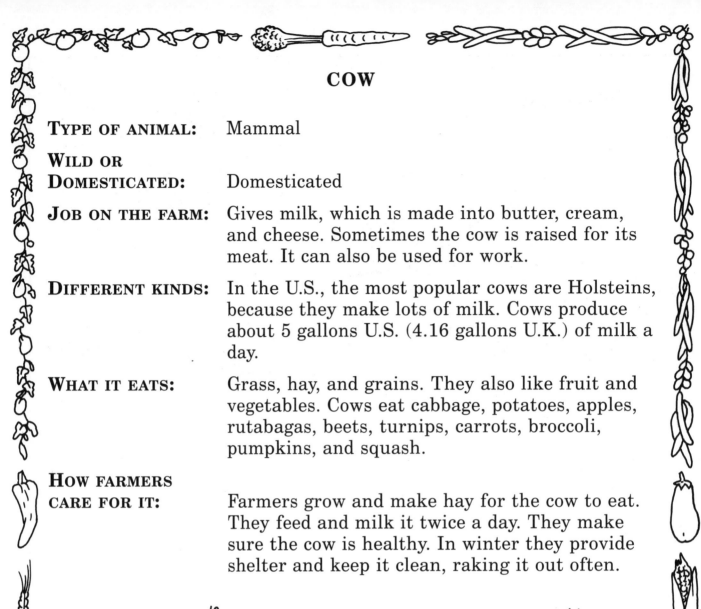

Ayrshire

Brown Swiss

Guernsey

Jersey

Here are some examples of different kinds of cows.

COYOTE

TYPE OF ANIMAL: Mammal

WILD OR DOMESTICATED: Wild

JOB ON THE FARM: Coyotes are a menace to the farm. They may attack the animals. But an even more serious threat are the diseases they may carry, which may even affect the farmer.

DIFFERENT KINDS: When coyotes interbreed with dogs, they make what people call "coy dogs."

WHAT IT EATS: Rabbits, field mice, fruit, vegetables, and anything it finds.

HOW FARMERS CARE FOR IT: Farmers keep livestock in safe pens, especially from dusk to dawn, when coyotes are most active. They also keep young livestock safely penned in at all times. Guard dogs can also be helpful in protecting the farm animals. Solid 6-foot (1.8m) fences will keep coyotes out of the farm as well.

These dog-like footprints are a sign that a coyote has been here.

CROW

TYPE OF ANIMAL:	Bird
WILD OR DOMESTICATED:	Wild
JOB ON THE FARM:	Usually crows are troublemakers on the farm, eating the crops. That's why farmers make scarecrows—to scare them away. But even though crows eat a lot of the farmer's grain, they also eat a lot of the insects that harm the crops. So they also do some good.
DIFFERENT KINDS:	Crows are probably the most intelligent of all birds. There are 31 different kinds of crow.
WHAT IT EATS:	Crows will eat anything edible, and many things that aren't. Their regular diet includes animal and vegetable matter, insects, crops (especially corn), and occasionally the eggs or young of other birds.
HOW FARMERS CARE FOR IT:	Farmers put up scarecrows in their fields, but because crows are so smart, any scarecrow that stays in the same place for more than a few days quickly becomes a perch. Farmers also keep cats to chase the crows away.

The raven is closely related to the crow, but it is larger and tends to live away from cities in wilder areas.

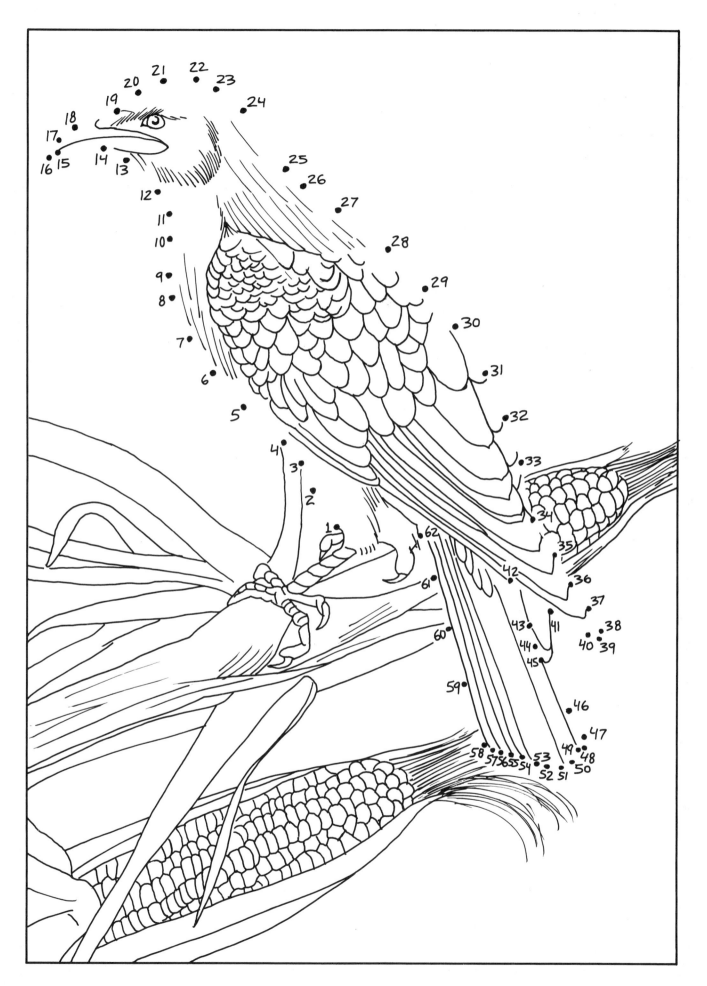

DOG

TYPE OF ANIMAL:	Mammal
WILD OR DOMESTICATED:	Domesticated
JOB ON THE FARM:	To help keep other animals from wandering away when they are in the fields and hills. They round up the flocks—of sheep, llamas, goats, alpacas, or cattle—and bring them home. Many people also keep dogs to guard their homes. Some dogs, like terriers, are also great rat catchers.
DIFFERENT KINDS:	There have been more than a thousand different breeds of dogs. Today about two hundred breeds are popular. German shepherds and English collies are used to help herd animals.
WHAT IT EATS:	The dog eats dog food, which is always some kind of meat.
HOW FARMERS CARE FOR IT:	Farmers feed it, wash it, train it, and give it affection. Very often they make sure the dog gets exercise.

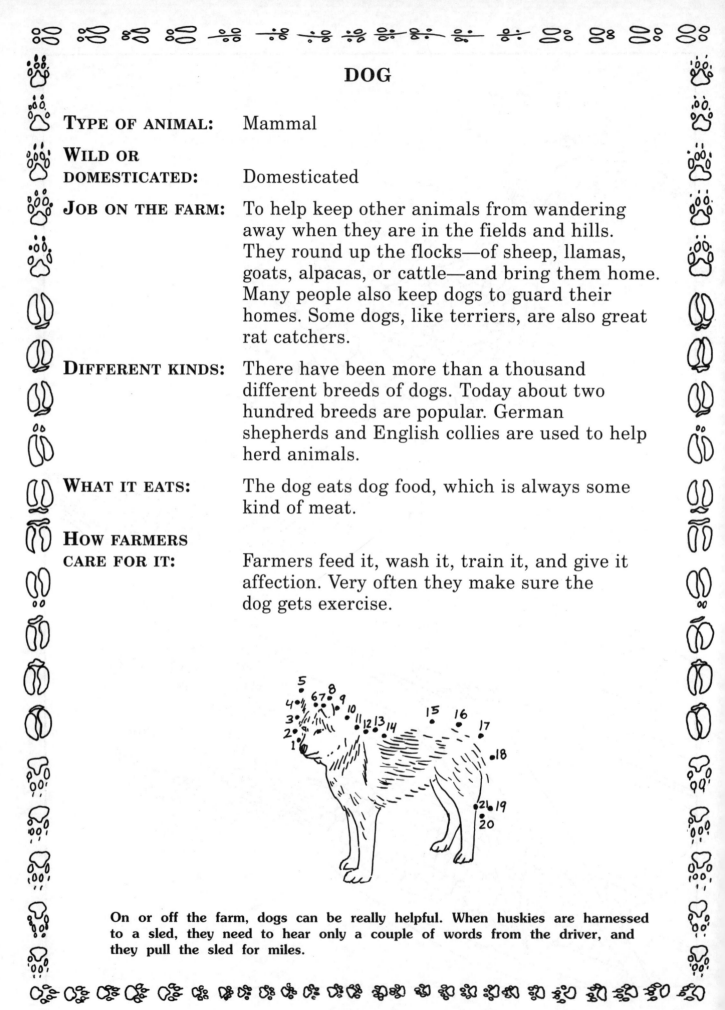

On or off the farm, dogs can be really helpful. When huskies are harnessed to a sled, they need to hear only a couple of words from the driver, and they pull the sled for miles.

DONKEY

TYPE OF ANIMAL:	Mammal
WILD OR DOMESTICATED:	Domesticated
JOB ON THE FARM:	Donkeys were first domesticated 6,000 years ago in Egypt. Slow and sure-footed, they are used to carry heavy things. They also protect sheep from predators.
DIFFERENT KINDS:	Donkeys, burros, and mules are all very similar. Donkeys are sometimes bred with horses; their offspring is an animal called a mule. Mules are bigger than donkeys, and stronger and heartier than horses. A burro is an everyday working donkey.
WHAT IT EATS:	It needs clean hay that is low in protein, since donkeys tend to be fat. Sometimes they are also fed grain.
HOW FARMERS CARE FOR IT:	The donkey needs a stall and a trough that are kept clean, food and water, and lots of attention. It is a very affectionate animal.

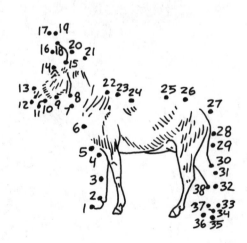

A mule's mother is a horse, and its father is a donkey.

DUCK

TYPE OF ANIMAL: Bird

WILD OR DOMESTICATED: Domesticated

JOB ON THE FARM: Laying eggs, providing meat, and giving feathers to make the down that fills blankets and pillows.

DIFFERENT KINDS: There are many different ducks from all over the world. Some are known as puddle ducks, and some are called diving ducks. Puddle ducks live in shallow marshes and rivers, while diving ducks live in large lakes and bays.

WHAT IT EATS: On the farm, mostly vegetables, but it may also be fed grain or acorns to fatten it up.

HOW FARMERS CARE FOR IT: A duck is a kind of waterfowl, which means that it needs water to live. A farmer may provide a pool of water and keep it fresh for the ducks, if there isn't a pond already there. He also needs to clean out their living space sometimes if it is enclosed.

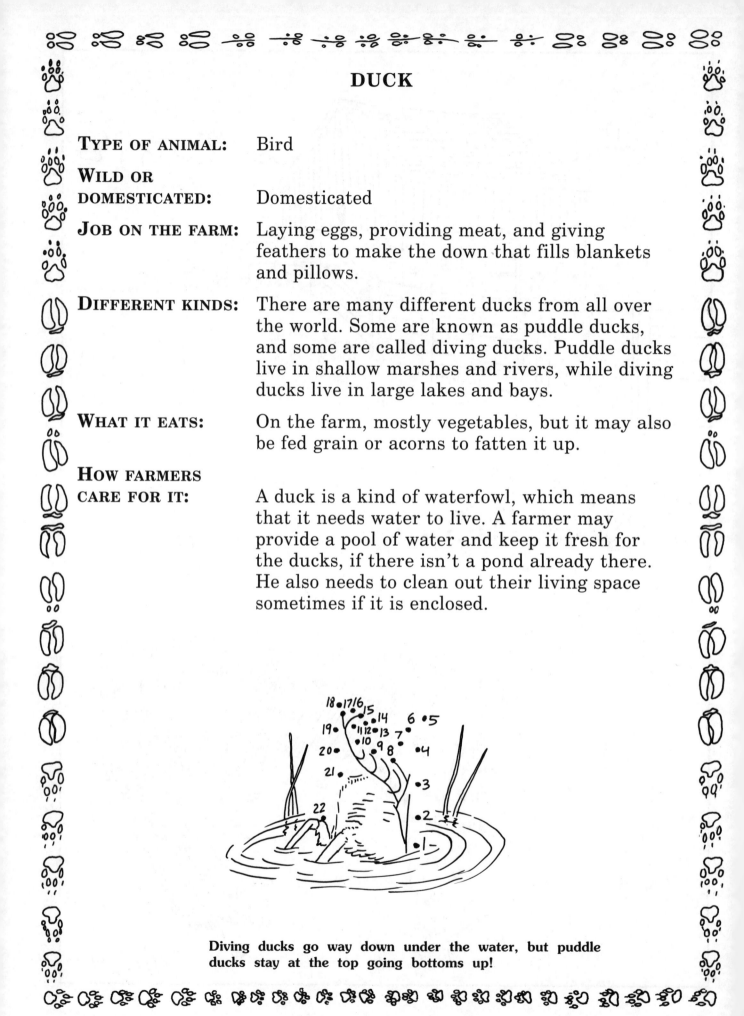

Diving ducks go way down under the water, but puddle ducks stay at the top going bottoms up!

ELK

TYPE OF ANIMAL: Mammal

WILD OR DOMESTICATED: Domesticated

JOB ON THE FARM: Elk have been raised by people as a business since 1900. There are elk ranches in many parts of the United States, in Canada, New Zealand, Australia, Russia, China, Korea, and Mexico. They are raised for meat and for the velvet that grows on their antlers, which can help treat illnesses in people.

DIFFERENT KINDS: North American, Manitoban, Rocky Mountain, and Tule elk are the types that are most often ranched.

WHAT IT EATS: High-protein alfalfa and grain.

HOW FARMERS CARE FOR IT: The elk needs land, fencing, and some kind of enclosed space. It needs to be fed and checked on a regular basis. You can run three elk in the same amount of space you would need for one cow. The elk eats up to 20 pounds (9kg) of feed a day.

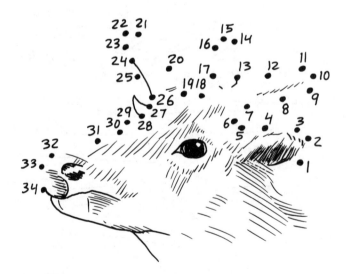

Bulls (male elk) produce antlers every year, and before they get hard, the antlers are velvety.

GOAT

TYPE OF ANIMAL:	Mammal
WILD OR DOMESTICATED:	Domesticated, but can be wild.
JOB ON THE FARM:	Goats have been used for thousands of years to provide milk, cheese, meat, fleece, and leather. Some are raised for their hair, which can be woven and used to make clothing. It's called mohair.
DIFFERENT KINDS:	Three common types found on farms are Nubian Goats, Nigerian Dwarf goats, and Pygmy goats. Nubians are large, have big floppy ears, and provide dairy products. Dwarf goats are medium-sized and also give milk; pygmy goats are the smallest and are often used for showing.
WHAT IT EATS:	Alfalfa, clover, and grass.
HOW FARMERS CARE FOR IT:	First of all, a farmer must keep at least two goats; one would be lonely. The goat needs shelter, but lots of air. It needs fresh food and water every day, and its house needs to be kept clean.

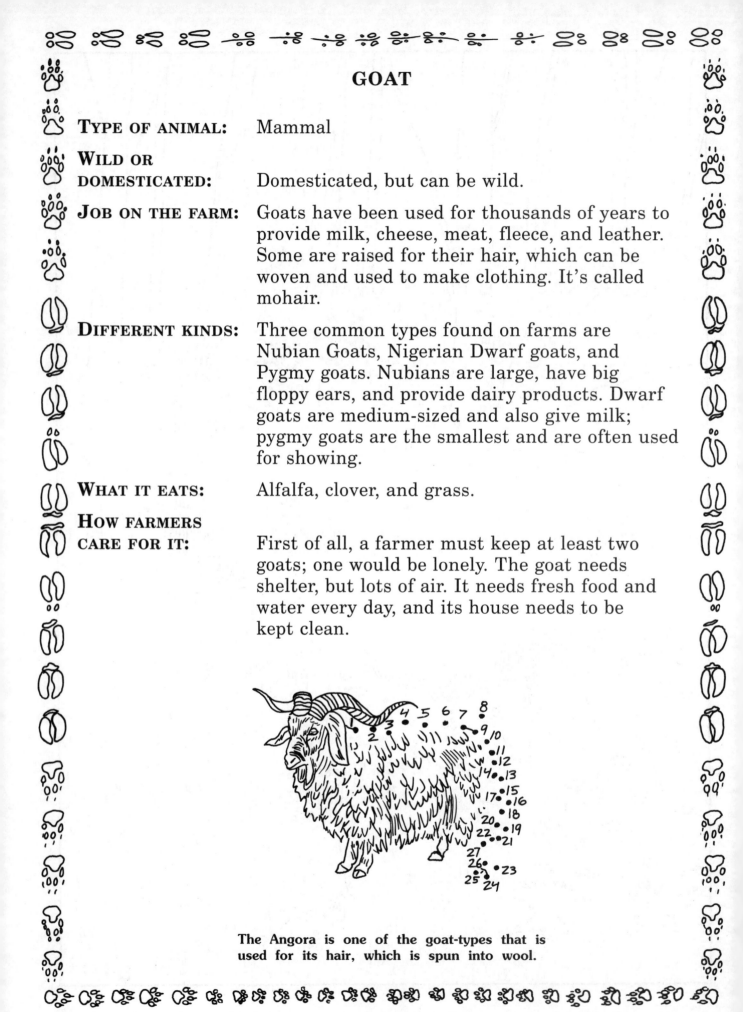

The Angora is one of the goat-types that is used for its hair, which is spun into wool.

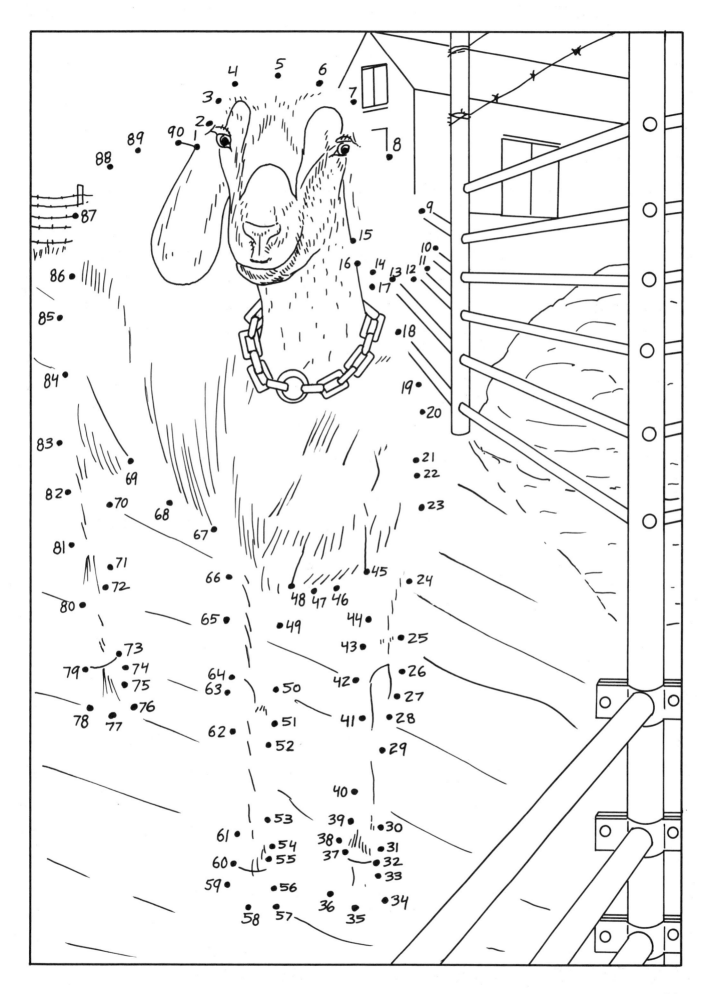

31

GOOSE

TYPE OF ANIMAL: Bird

**WILD OR
DOMESTICATED:**   Domesticated

JOB ON THE FARM: To make eggs, to provide feathers for down, and to be used for meat. Geese make good watchdogs too, with their high-spirited honking when strangers come around. Some of them may be able to help do weeding in the garden.

DIFFERENT KINDS: There are many breeds of goose. One is called the "Swan Goose," and can be brown or white with a big knob on its bill.

WHAT IT EATS: Greens—meaning grass, alfalfa, and chard—and grain.

**HOW FARMERS
CARE FOR IT:**   Clean, fresh water must be available at all times. The farmer needs to provide a shelter that is waterproof, predator-proof, and has lots of air. The bedding must be changed daily, and the area cleaned weekly. Geese also need a roost, like a bale of straw, to sleep on.

**A gosling is a baby goose, and the mother goose and a
gander (a male goose) raise their babies together.**

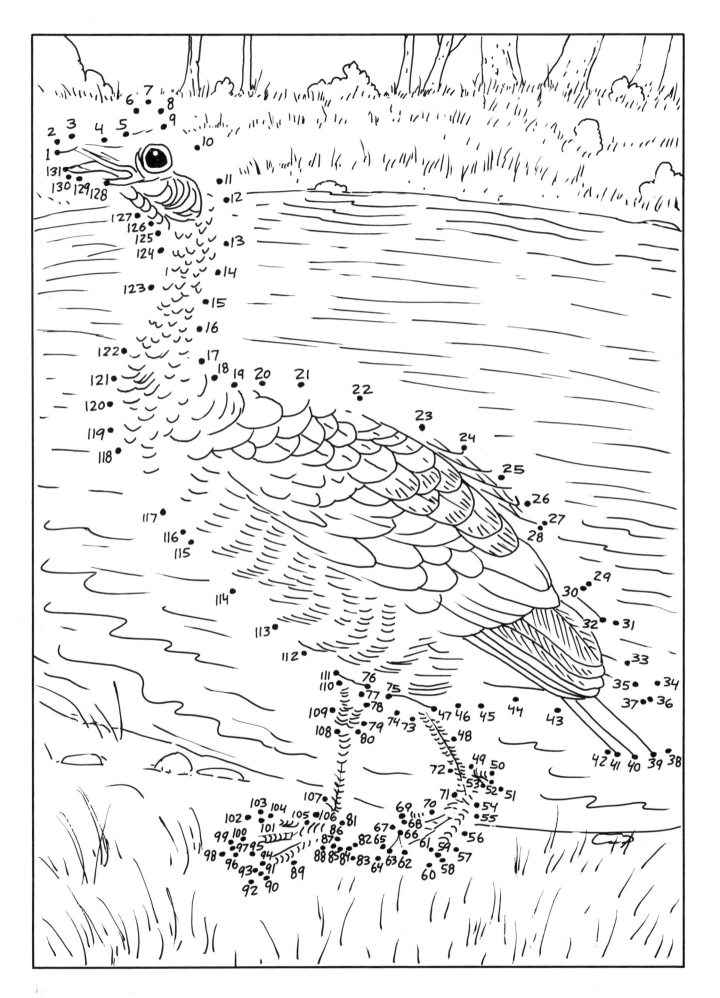

GROUNDHOG

TYPE OF ANIMAL: Mammal

WILD OR DOMESTICATED: Wild

JOB ON THE FARM: A groundhog can be a help and a "hurt" to the farm. Because it burrows, making its home in holes underground, it helps other small animals by giving them places to hide. On the other hand, the groundhog can do a lot of damage to crops.

DIFFERENT KINDS: Also known as a woodchuck or a whistle pig, the groundhog is a rodent, and its closest relative is the squirrel. Groundhog hair is used by fishermen for tying trout flies.

WHAT IT EATS: In the wild it eats dandelion greens, clover, plantain herbs, and grasses. It also likes garden vegetables.

HOW FARMERS CARE FOR IT: Because groundhogs can damage crops, they are considered pests on a farm.

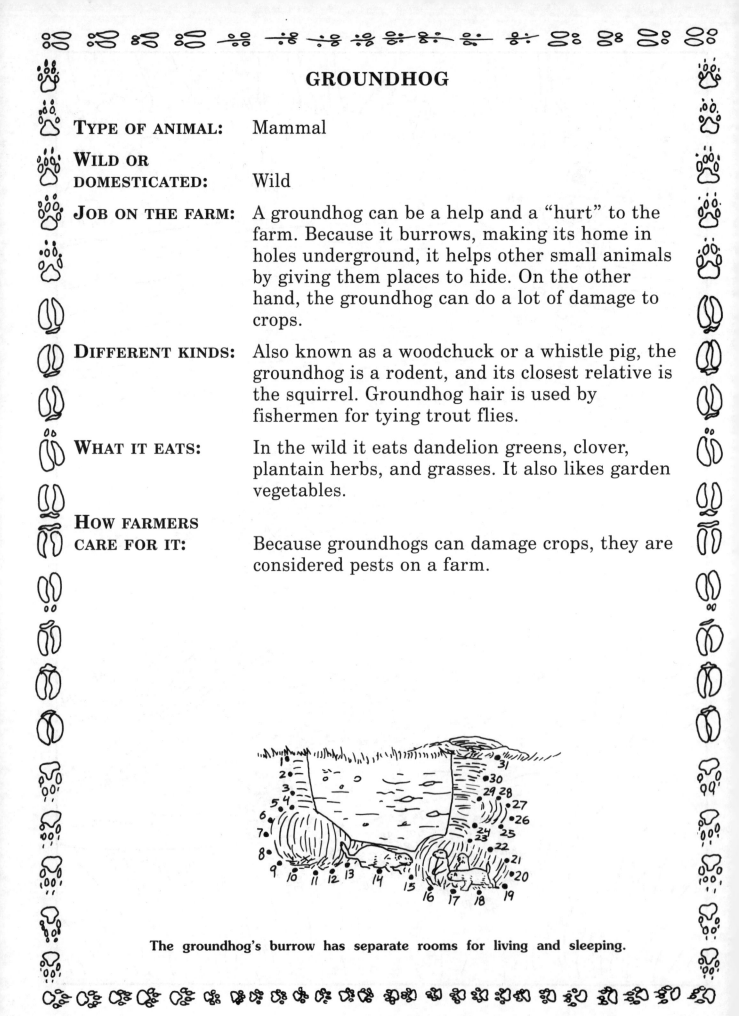

The groundhog's burrow has separate rooms for living and sleeping.

HAWK

TYPE OF ANIMAL:	Bird
WILD OR DOMESTICATED:	Wild
JOB ON THE FARM:	Hawks are not kept on a farm, but they do often appear, since they live on every continent except Antartica. They can be a help to the farmer because they prey on small mammals and insects that are pests to a farm.
DIFFERENT KINDS:	The hawk family includes hawks, eagles, kites, ospreys, and vultures.
WHAT IT EATS:	Small mammals, reptiles, fish, insects, and other birds.
HOW FARMERS CARE FOR IT:	Farmers generally don't do anything for hawks. But since DDT, a pesticide used in farming, is no longer used, there are many more hawks around.

Many hawks don't build a nest but find cavities in rotten trees. Here is a nest of hawk eggs that was found in the grass.

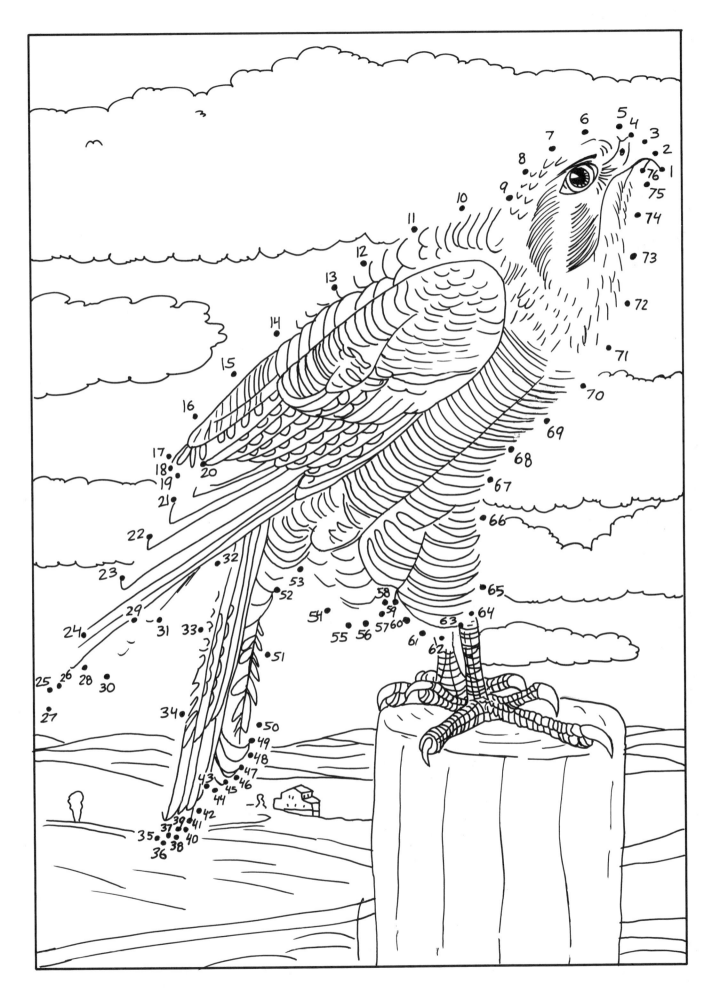

HEN

TYPE OF ANIMAL: Bird

WILD OR DOMESTICATED: Domesticated

JOB ON THE FARM: A hen is a female chicken and is raised for its eggs and meat.

DIFFERENT KINDS: Chickens have been sharing our lives since at least 3250 B.C. They come in all shapes and sizes and colors. Some varieties lay eggs that are different colors too, such as green, blue, pink, or brown. Chickens have been bred to lay white ones, because people seemed to like white the best. Today the average hen lays 300 eggs a year. Her wild ancestor, the jungle fowl, would have laid only 10–20 eggs per year.

WHAT IT EATS: Insects, worms, fruit, seeds, acorns, grains, slugs, snails, and many other foods.

HOW FARMERS CARE FOR IT: The chicken needs a coop or henhouse to live in. A henhouse is a small house that has an area for breeding, one for brooding—which means laying and hatching eggs—and one for raising chicks. It needs to be fed, given water, and cleaned up after. It needs to be protected from predators by being fenced in, but it also needs room to roam.

A hen will lay a lot of eggs in a year, almost one a day!

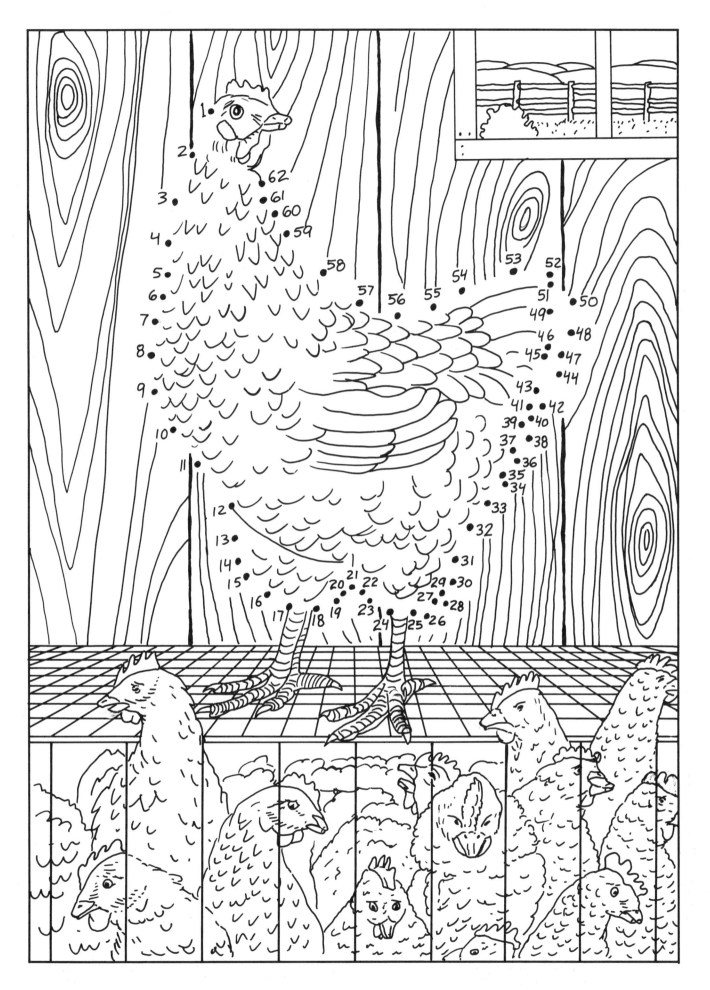

HORSE

TYPE OF ANIMAL: Mammal

WILD OR DOMESTICATED: Domesticated

JOB ON THE FARM: People began to tame horses over 4,000 years ago. Horses pull plows, carts, and heavy wagons, and also help round up animals like cows, sheep, and other horses. They give rides when needed for work or fun.

DIFFERENT KINDS: Draft horses are the most commonly used for work. They pull everything from wagons to plows to logs. They used to be the farmer's main way to plow his fields and haul his goods. Belgians and Percherons are two breeds of horses.

WHAT IT EATS: Grass, hay, grains.

HOW FARMERS CARE FOR IT: A farmer will care for a horse by brushing it, cleaning off the dirt, cleaning its hooves, feeding it, and riding it. All horses need exercise.

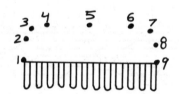
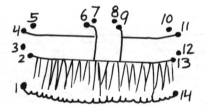
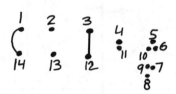

There are many tools used for grooming a horse.

LLAMA

TYPE OF ANIMAL: Mammal

WILD OR DOMESTICATED: Domesticated

JOB ON THE FARM: They work as pack animals; their hair is used as fiber for rugs and rope, and they are also used for meat. Llama dung is even put to use as fuel!

DIFFERENT KINDS: Llamas are about the size of a small horse but a good deal thinner. They have two wild cousins called the guanaco and the vicuna. Since llamas developed at high altitudes, they have a large lung capacity and an ability to use oxygen in the blood more efficiently than other animals.

WHAT IT EATS: Grass, trees, bushes. It also likes hay and grain.

HOW FARMERS CARE FOR IT: It needs land to graze on, shelter, and clean, fresh water. There should also be fencing to keep out predators such as dogs. The llama needs its toenails clipped every few months or so to prevent lameness.

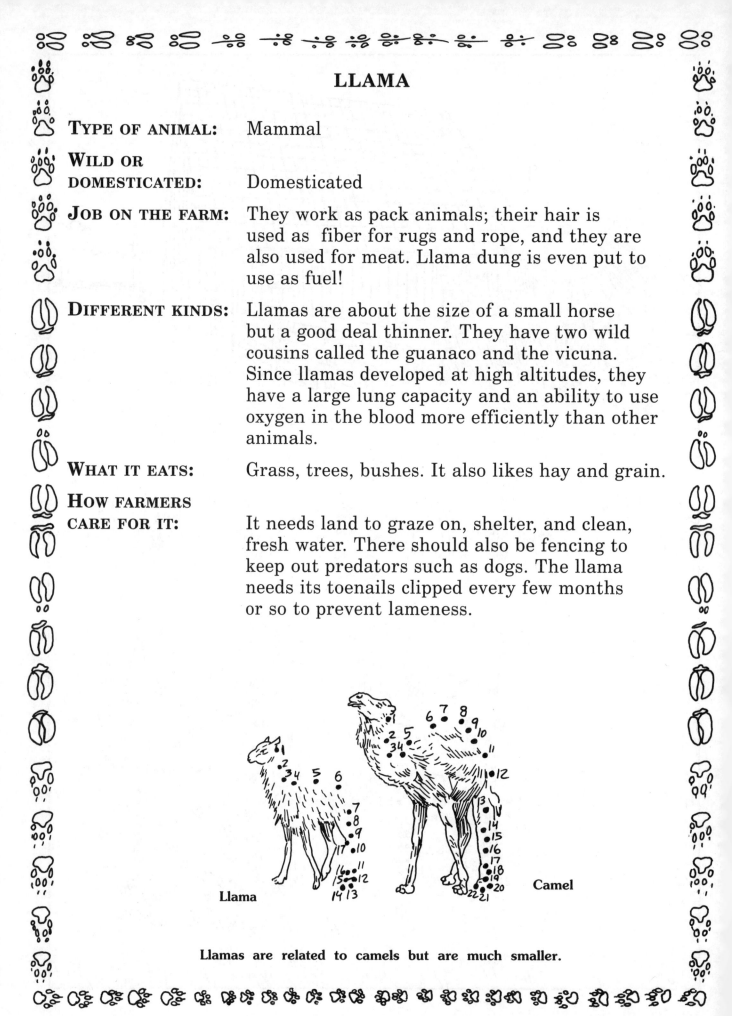

Llamas are related to camels but are much smaller.

43

MOUSE

TYPE OF ANIMAL:	Mammal
WILD OR DOMESTICATED:	Can be either.
JOB ON THE FARM:	Generally mice are pests on the farm, and farmers encourage cats and owls to rid them of these little critters. But there are some places where people breed mice to sell as pets.
DIFFERENT KINDS:	The most common type of mouse you might find on the farm is the Eastern or Western Harvest mouse. It is small and dainty; its fur is soft, and it is usually brown on top with a white underbelly and a very long tail.
WHAT IT EATS:	In the wild, the mouse eats various vegetables, plants, and seeds. Sometimes it will eat bugs.
HOW FARMERS CARE FOR IT:	A farmer will often have cats on the farm to help keep mice away.

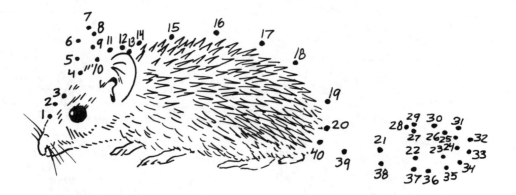

Spiny mice have pointy spines on them, but the spines don't sting. They are also the one kind of mouse that doesn't have a sense of smell.

OSTRICH

TYPE OF ANIMAL:	Bird
WILD OR DOMESTICATED:	Domesticated
JOB ON THE FARM:	To provide eggs, feathers, meat, and leather. Its eggs are so big that to hard-boil them takes 1½ hours.
DIFFERENT KINDS:	There are three breeds of ostrich: African Black, African Blueneck, and African Redneck. They are native to Africa and the largest of all birds. They lay the largest eggs.
WHAT IT EATS:	The ostrich eats about 4 pounds (1.8kg) of alfalfa pellets and hay each day. It does not like to be watched while it eats.
HOW FARMERS CARE FOR IT:	Farmers feed and groom it.

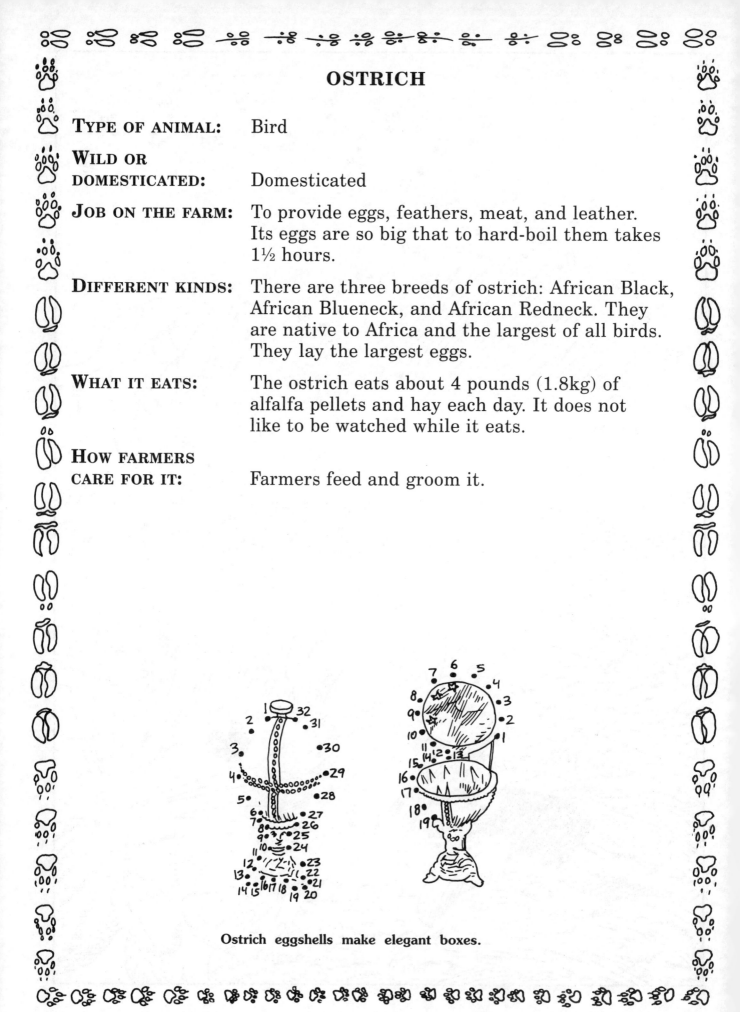

Ostrich eggshells make elegant boxes.

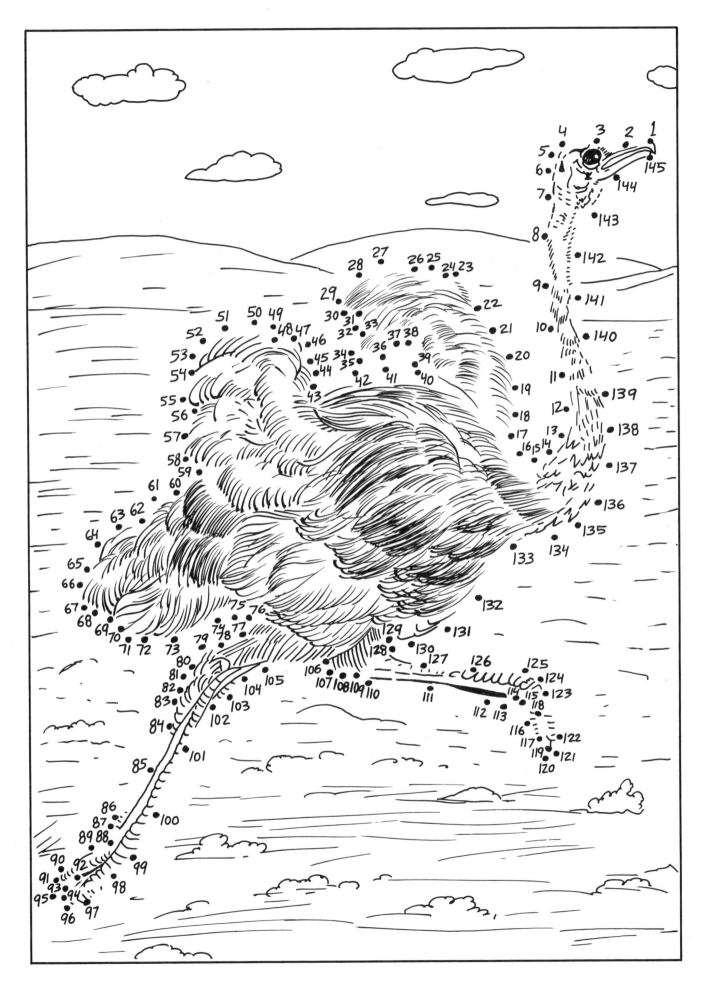

OWL

TYPE OF ANIMAL:	Bird
WILD OR DOMESTICATED:	Wild
JOB ON THE FARM:	To get rid of mice and rats by feeding on them. Owls hunt at night, using especially their sense of hearing to find their prey as they move in the dark.
DIFFERENT KINDS:	There are many different types of owl. The barn owl breeds in North America. The eagle owl lives on the edge of forests in Europe. The most powerful owl is the great horned owl; it also lives in North America.
WHAT IT EATS:	Rodents, insects, frogs, and birds.
HOW FARMERS CARE FOR IT:	Some farmers encourage owls to nest in their barns.

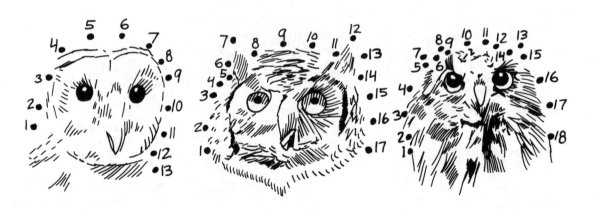

Barn owl   Horned owl   Eagle owl

Different owls have different faces.

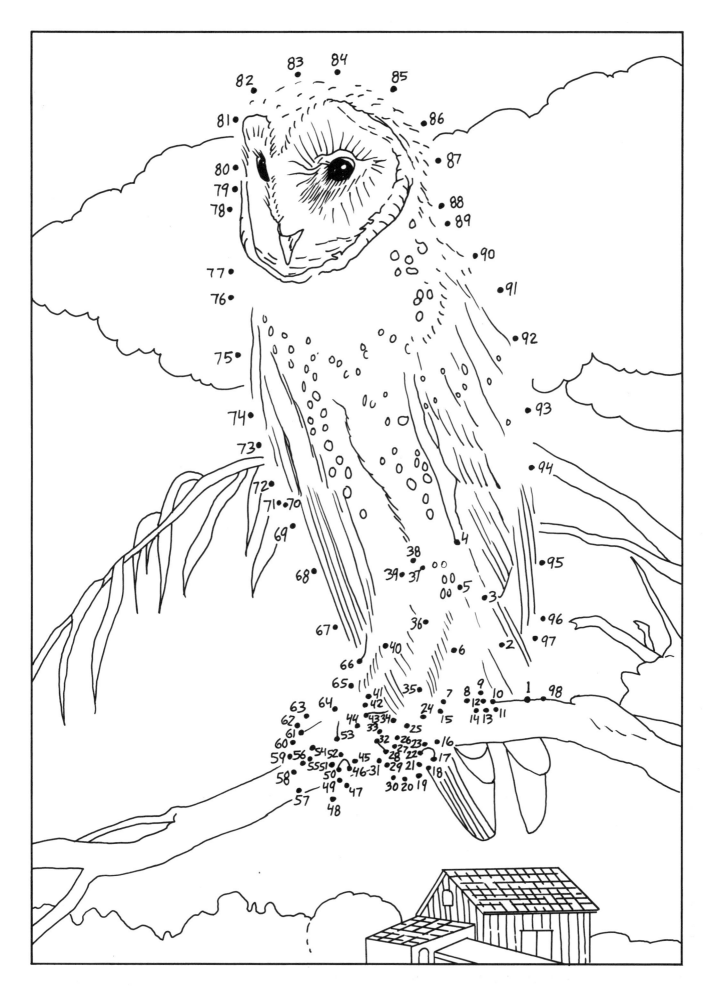

49

OX

TYPE OF ANIMAL:	Mammal
WILD OR DOMESTICATED:	Domesticated
JOB ON THE FARM:	Incredibly strong animals, oxen are used for work, very much like draft horses. They can plow fields, pull logs, remove stumps, and pull wagons. Some are used for work; others are raised for their meat, milk, and hides.
DIFFERENT KINDS:	The ox is a relative of the water buffalo. The females are milked, and the males do the hard work.
WHAT IT EATS:	Grass, leaves off trees, and woody plants.
HOW FARMERS CARE FOR IT:	Farmers feed oxen, and provide lots of space for them to live and to graze. When grass is scarce, farmers give them hay.

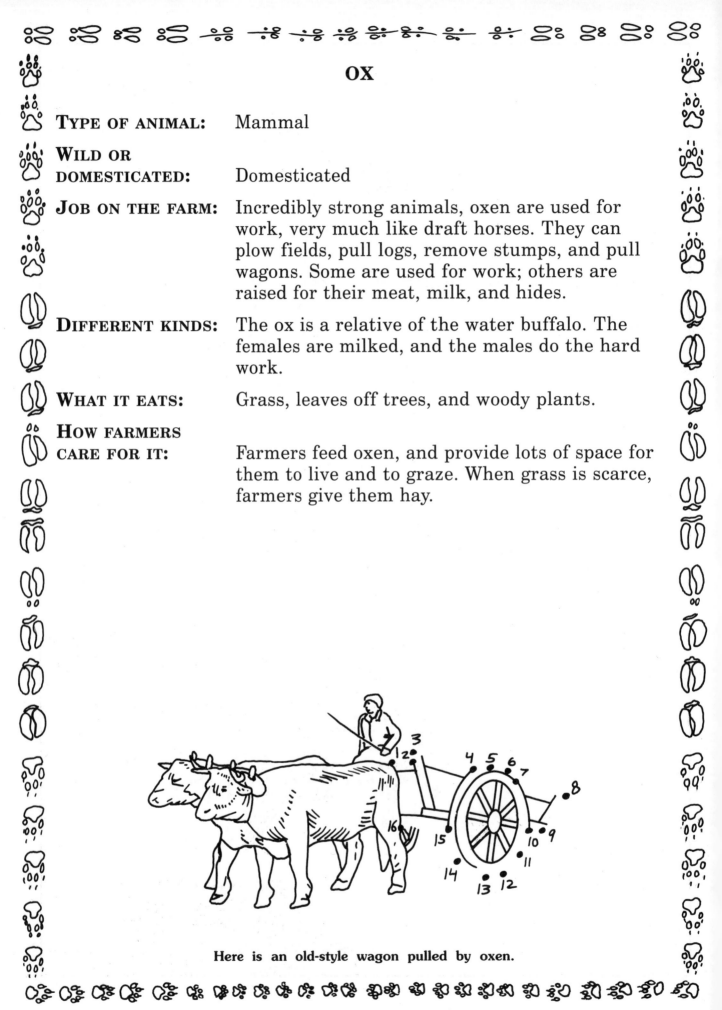

Here is an old-style wagon pulled by oxen.

PIG

TYPE OF ANIMAL: Mammal

WILD OR DOMESTICATED: Domesticated

JOB ON THE FARM: To give food and hides. It is believed that people started taming pigs about 8,000 years ago. Some pigs never go to market. They are kept for showing. There are about 800 million pigs in the world that are tame or used to living with people. Pigs are the smartest of all farm animals—some scientists say even smarter than dogs—and some even come when they're called.

DIFFERENT KINDS: There are about 300 different types of pigs, but they all have the same basic characteristics—a heavy, round, bristly-skinned body with a round flat nose called a snout. Some are spotted, pink, black, or brown.

HOW FARMERS CARE FOR IT: Farmers provide food and shelter and water to get wet in. The pig likes to stay clean and also needs to wet its skin when it's hot; otherwise it gets sick.

The wild boar is the animal from which all pigs are descended.

QUAIL

TYPE OF ANIMAL: Bird

WILD OR DOMESTICATED: Domesticated

JOB ON THE FARM: Quail are originally from Asia, domesticated in Japan in the 11th century as songbirds. Their meat and eggs became popular as time went by. An adult hen will lay over 300 eggs a year, and each hen's egg has a unique color pattern, shape, and size.

DIFFERENT KINDS: The most common type of quail is the European quail. The Japanese quail is known as *Coturnix japonica*.

WHAT IT EATS: Half of a quail's diet is insects and the other half is vegetation. On the farm, though, they are given feed that has turkey in it.

HOW FARMERS CARE FOR IT: The quail needs food, water, and cage space. It also needs to be kept fairly warm.

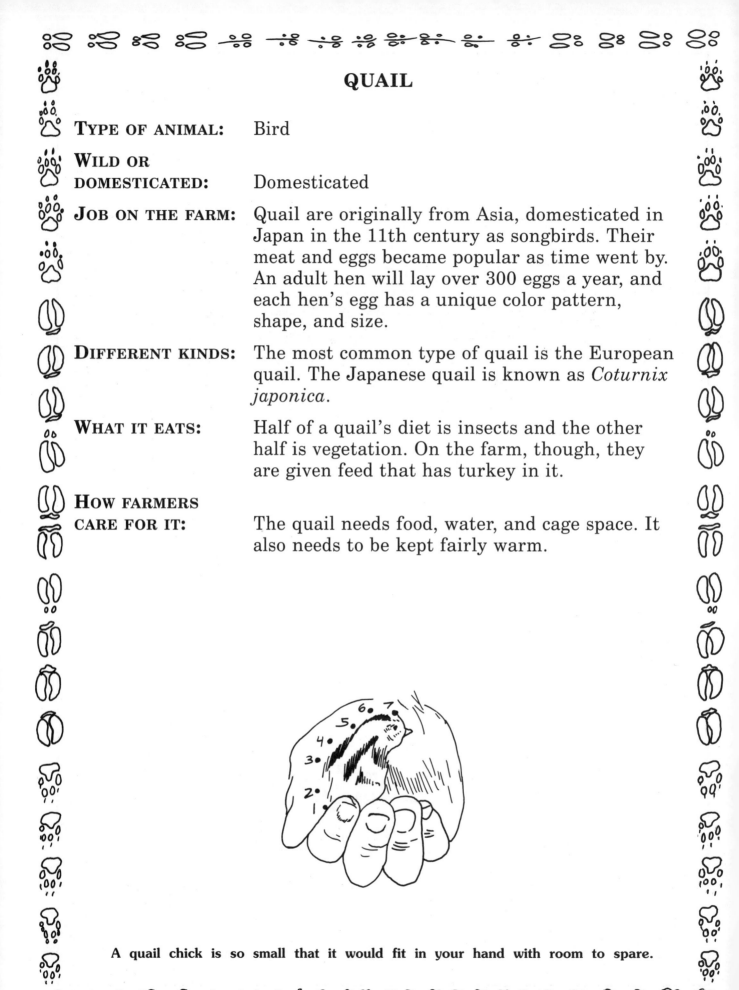

A quail chick is so small that it would fit in your hand with room to spare.

RABBIT

TYPE OF ANIMAL: Mammal

WILD OR DOMESTICATED: Domesticated

JOB ON THE FARM: A rabbit's job on the farm is usually to provide meat.

DIFFERENT KINDS: There are many, many breeds of rabbit, some with longer or shorter fur, and all different colors, like brown, black, gray, white—and even lilac.

WHAT IT EATS: Rabbits eat rabbit pellets, a dried rabbit food made mostly of alfalfa, hay, grains, and of course, carrots!

HOW FARMERS CARE FOR IT: The rabbit is kept in a cage, and the cage needs to be kept clean. Every day it is given water and food.

The Angora rabbit has very long fur that is sometimes used to make sweaters that are amazingly soft.

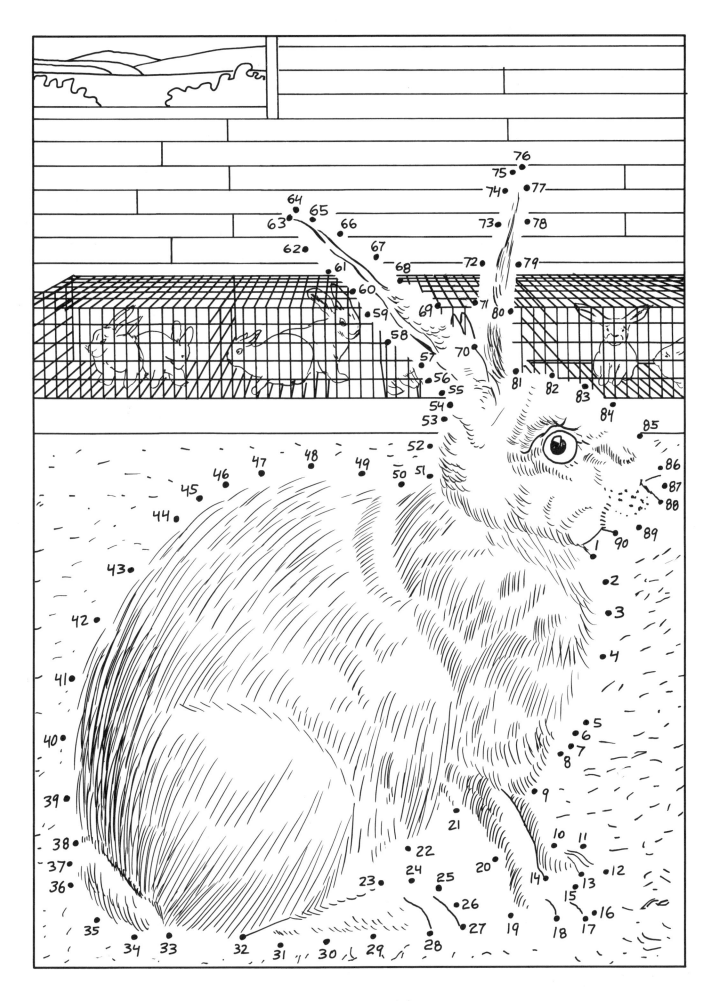

RAM

TYPE OF ANIMAL: Mammal

WILD OR DOMESTICATED: Domesticated

JOB ON THE FARM: People started raising sheep, which provide both meat and clothing, over 10,000 years ago. The ram is a male sheep and is brought in with the females to help make baby sheep or lambs.

DIFFERENT KINDS: There are many different kinds of ram. Some are raised mainly for their meat and others for their wool.

WHAT IT EATS: Grass and hay.

HOW FARMERS CARE FOR IT: The most important thing a farmer can do for a sheep is to keep it safe from predators—animals like coyotes, wolves, and dogs. Sometimes a farmer will put larger animals like mules or llamas in the pasture to help scare off predators.

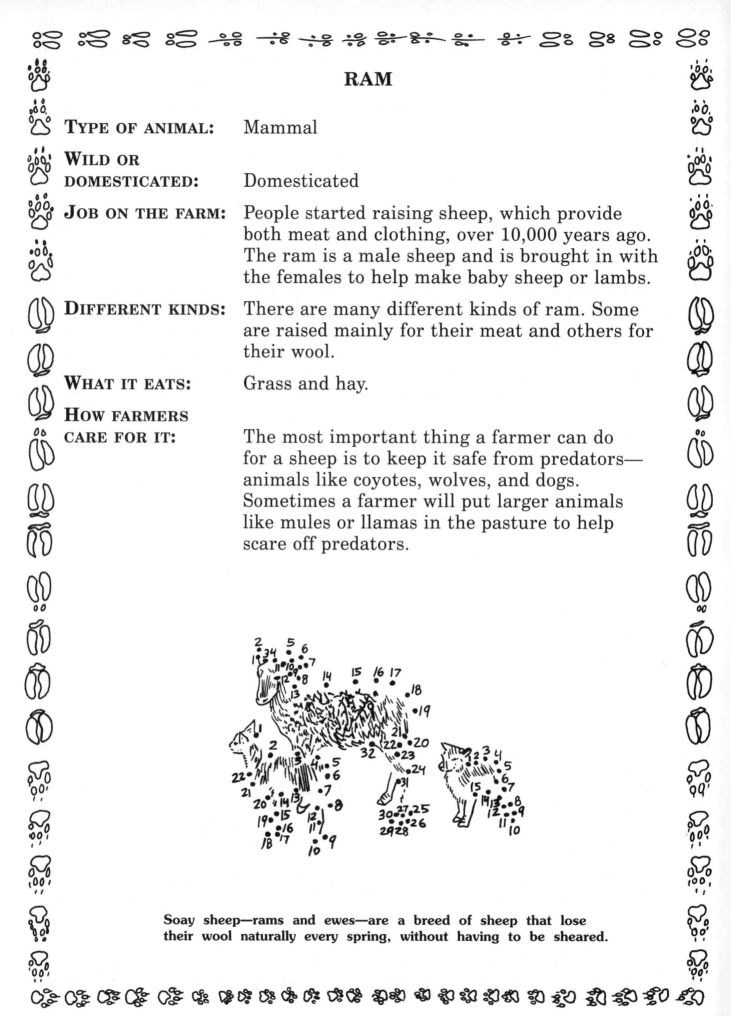

Soay sheep—rams and ewes—are a breed of sheep that lose their wool naturally every spring, without having to be sheared.

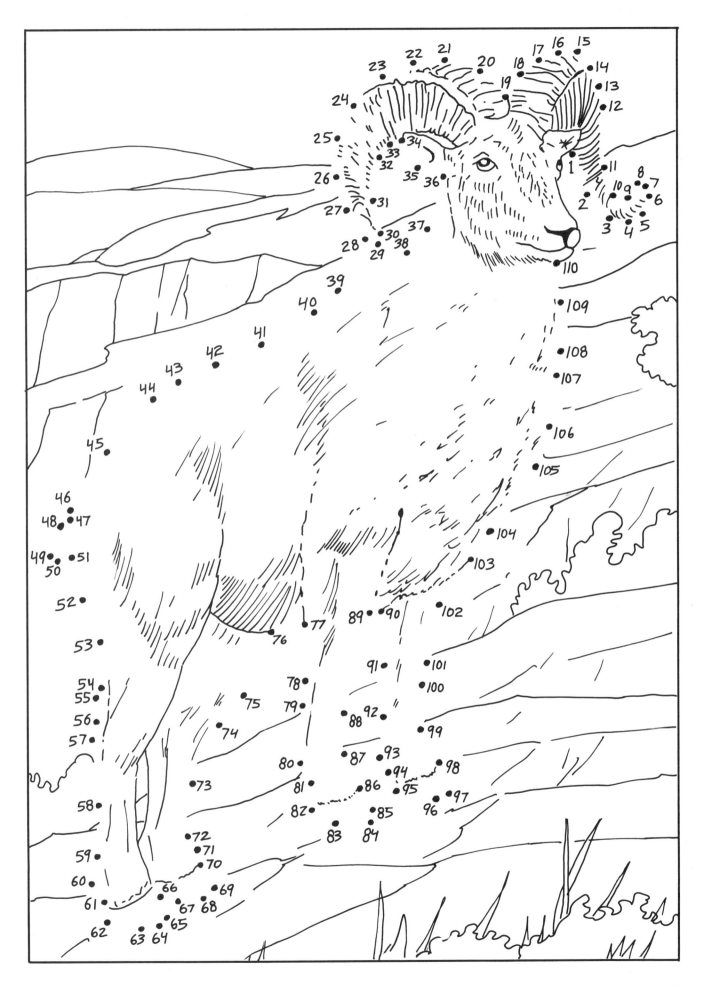

59

RAT

TYPE OF ANIMAL: Mammal

WILD OR DOMESTICATED: Can be either.

JOB ON THE FARM: Rats, like mice, are considered pests on the farm. They chew through wood and wire and damage stores of grain.

DIFFERENT KINDS: Most rats look very much alike, but some have no tail and others are miniature—about half the size of a normal rat, which is 7 to 10 inches (17.5 to 25cm) long.

WHAT IT EATS: Rats are omnivores, which means that they eat vegetables and meat. Wild rats eat whatever they can find. They will even eat smaller rodents as "snacks."

HOW FARMERS CARE FOR IT: Most farmers will "take care" of rats by having a cat that will hunt them.

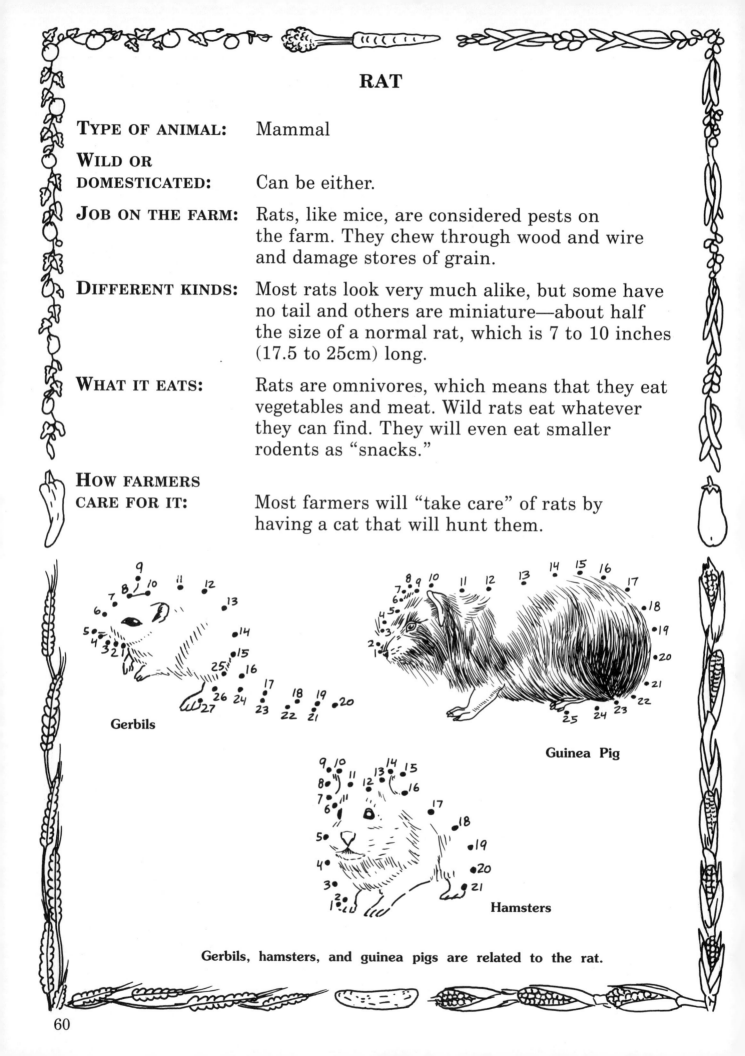

Gerbils

Guinea Pig

Hamsters

Gerbils, hamsters, and guinea pigs are related to the rat.

60

REINDEER

TYPE OF ANIMAL: Mammal

WILD OR DOMESTIC: Wild

JOB ON THE FARM: Reindeer can be trained to pull sleds or carts and give rides. Often they are raised for their meat and antlers; the velvet on their antlers can be used as medicine. Both males and females grow antlers.

DIFFERENT KINDS: Reindeer and caribou are the same species, but reindeer are domesticated and caribou are not. People tamed wild caribou at least 5,000 years ago in Europe and Asia. Now the Sami (or Lapps) in Scandinavia depend for their livelihood on raising reindeer. There are over 2 million reindeer in Russia.

WHAT IT EATS: Grains and hay. In the wild, their favorite food is mushrooms.

HOW FARMERS CARE FOR IT: Farmers provide shelter, food, and water. The reindeer needs a fence to keep it in and predators out. It also needs food and water, but in winter it prefers snow to water.

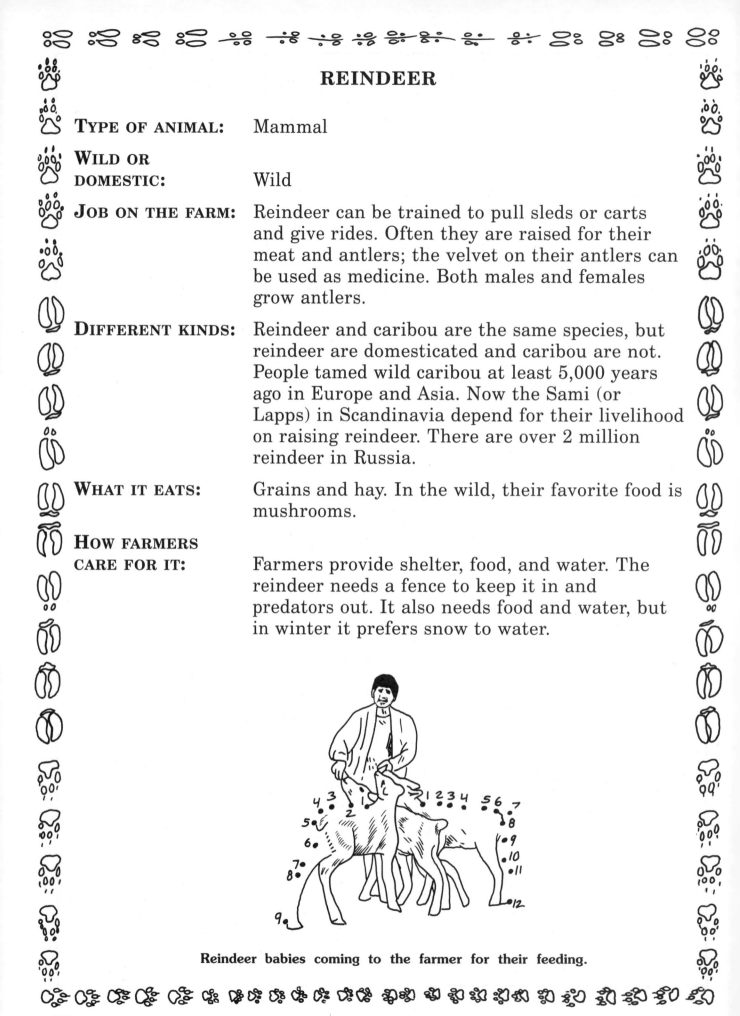

Reindeer babies coming to the farmer for their feeding.

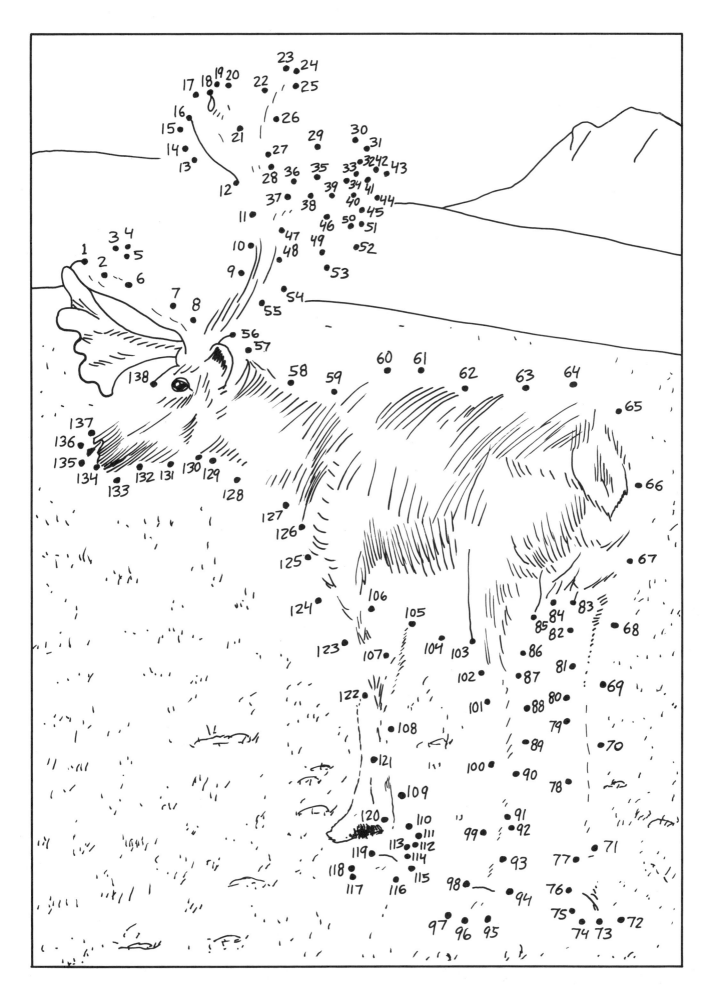

ROOSTER

TYPE OF ANIMAL:	Bird
WILD OR DOMESTICATED:	Domesticated
JOB ON THE FARM:	To wake up the people and the animals on the farm. They also mate with hens to make baby chicks.
DIFFERENT KINDS:	A rooster is a male chicken. He is more brightly colored than the hen, and has a larger comb— the "hat" on his head. There are many different breeds that are different sizes and colors.
WHAT IT EATS:	Insects, worms, fruit, seeds, acorns, grains, slugs, snails, and many other foods.
HOW FARMERS CARE FOR IT:	Roosters need food, water, a clean coop, and a roaming area that is fenced in.

A Silkie is a type of fowl that has fur instead of feathers. The Silkie hens will take care of another bird's eggs.

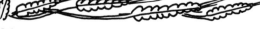

SHEEP

TYPE OF ANIMAL: Mammal

WILD OR DOMESTICATED: Domesticated

JOB ON THE FARM: To give wool, milk, and meat. As much as 7 to 10 pounds (3 to 4.5kg) of wool can be shorn from the largest sheep. That's enough to make a grown man's suit, and one pound (0.5kg) of wool can be spun into 20 miles (32km) of fine yarn.

DIFFERENT KINDS: Merino sheep originally came from Spain and give the best wool because it is so soft. Mountain sheep produce coarse short hair. This wool is used to make carpets and cheaper woolen suits and socks.

WHAT IT EATS: Grass, hay, and grains.

HOW FARMERS CARE FOR IT: Each spring, a sheep's wool is shaved off. This does not hurt it at all. The wool is spun to make yarn for knitting and weaving. A sheep needs land to graze on, since it eats mostly grass.

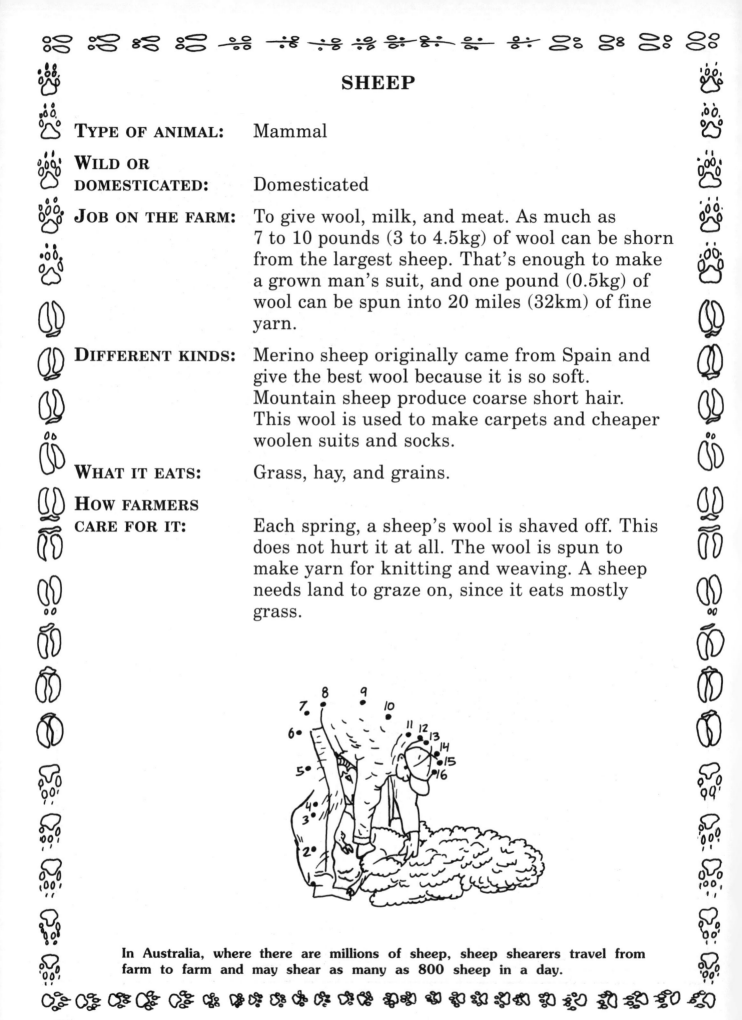

In Australia, where there are millions of sheep, sheep shearers travel from farm to farm and may shear as many as 800 sheep in a day.

SPIDER

TYPE OF ANIMAL: Not an insect—but an arthropod (meaning having jointed feet)

WILD OR DOMESTICATED: Wild

JOB ON THE FARM: A spider's job on the farm and in the world is to eat insects like mosquitoes that "bug" the animals. There are also farms where Golden Orb spiders are kept so that people can collect their silk. In these farms the spiders are well fed and protected from predators.

DIFFERENT KINDS: There are about 35,000 species of spider in the world. They live almost everywhere except in the polar regions and the oceans. The Golden Orb spider makes the strongest natural fiber known to man. People "milk" the spider for 15 minutes every day and get 49 yards (45m) of silk, and this process doesn't hurt the spider.

WHAT IT EATS: The Golden Orb spider makes a web strong enough to catch small birds, but it only eats small insects. That's the case with most spiders.

HOW FARMERS CARE FOR IT: Farmers make sure the spiders are protected from predators. The farmer milks the spiders for silk every day.

Spider silk is a lot like fish wire.

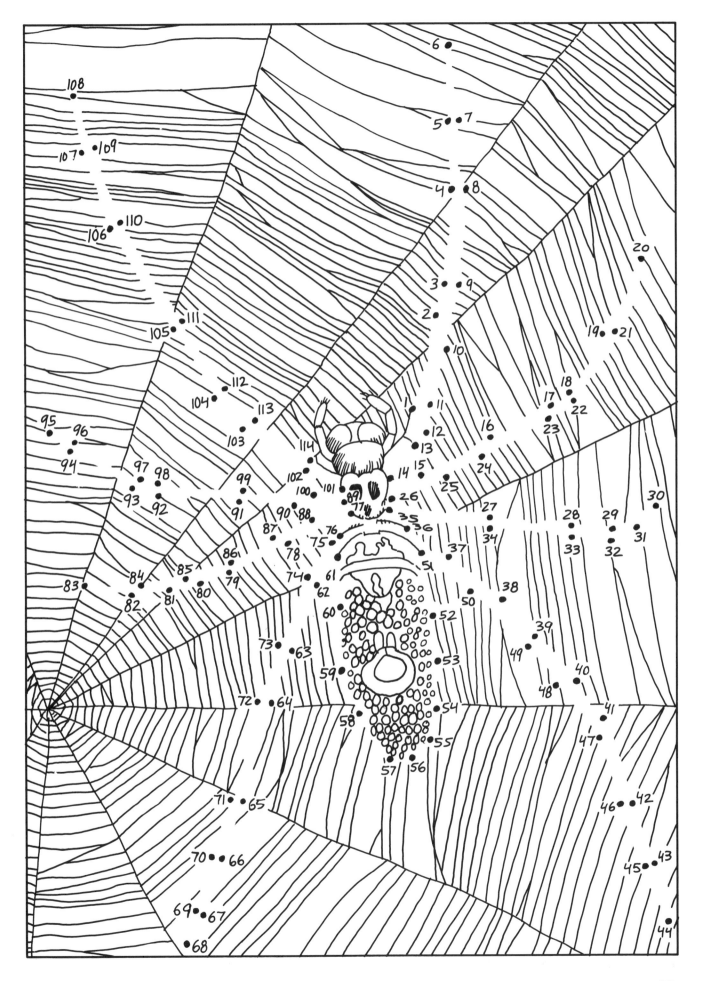

TROUT

TYPE OF ANIMAL:	Fish
WILD OR DOMESTICATED:	Wild
JOB ON THE FARM:	To make more trout and to be raised for food. Some farms produce as much as 88 tons (80 metric tonnes) of trout a year. Many farms invite people to fish in their ponds.
DIFFERENT KINDS:	The trout is a member of the salmon family of freshwater fish. There are Rainbow Trout, Brown Trout, Golden Trout, American Brook Trout, and hybrid varieties like Tiger, Zebra, and Leopard Trout.
WHAT IT EATS:	Phytoplankton, zooplankton, aquatic insects, fish eggs, mollusks, crustaceans, worms, leeches, batrachians, and fish. The feed that they are given on the farm is usually a high-quality fish meal.
HOW FARMERS CARE FOR IT:	Trout are hatched by farmers, who incubate the eggs. Soon they are put in the ponds. The fish on the farm are fed both by hand and by automatic hopper, which is operated by the fish themselves.

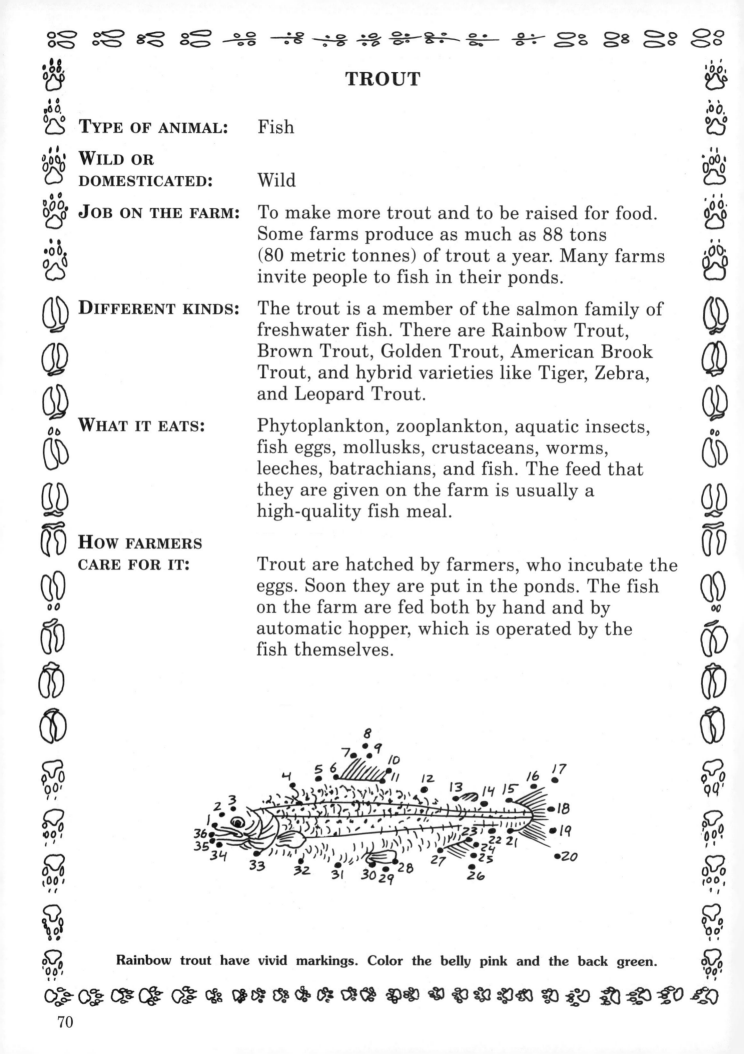

Rainbow trout have vivid markings. Color the belly pink and the back green.

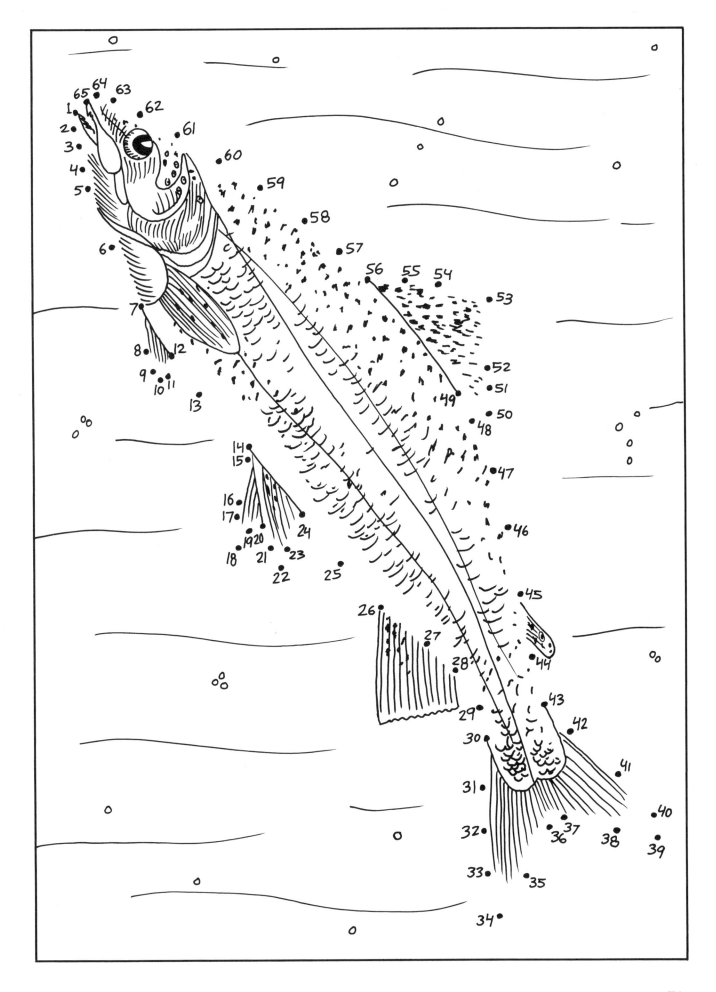

TURKEY

TYPE OF ANIMAL: Bird

WILD OR DOMESTICATED: Domesticated

JOB ON THE FARM: Turkeys are raised for their meat.

DIFFERENT KINDS: Turkeys come from North America; they were domesticated by the Aztecs in Mexico 500 years ago. Now they are bred throughout much of the world.

WHAT IT EATS: Grass, alfalfa, grain sprouts, lettuce, and swiss chard; mixed grains like corn, oats, and wheat, as well as a bit of grit and sunflower seeds. Turkeys also really like fruit.

HOW FARMERS CARE FOR IT: Farmers feed the turkey, give it lots of fresh water, and a clean shelter. It has to be fenced in, primarily to keep predators out.

Peacocks were raised for food by the Romans and in Medieval Europe, but, once discovered in the New World, turkeys became much more popular.

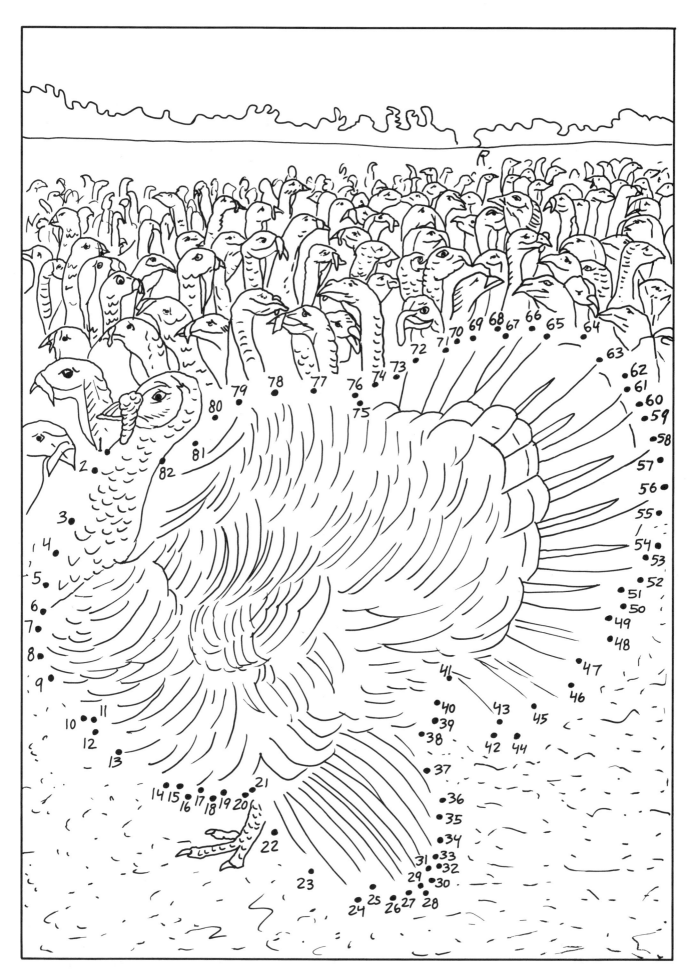

WATER BUFFALO

TYPE OF ANIMAL: Mammal

WILD OR DOMESTICATED: Domesticated

JOB ON THE FARM: The water buffalo is one of the most popular domestic animals in Southeast Asia. It helps in the wet rice paddies where a tractor cannot go. Even though the buffalo is heavy, it has wide feet that help it move across the water-logged soil. Water buffaloes are also kept for milk, meat, and leather.

DIFFERENT KINDS: There are two basic types of water buffalo: swamp buffalo and river water buffalo. They are found in Europe, Asia, Africa, Pakistan, Turkey, and Afghanistan. There is also a species of wild water buffalo that lives in Australia.

WHAT IT EATS: Water plants, grass, and ferns.

HOW FARMERS CARE FOR IT: Farmers provide fenced-in yards with shade and water for drinking and keeping the buffalo cool. Sometimes they remove the animal's horns so that it is easier to handle.

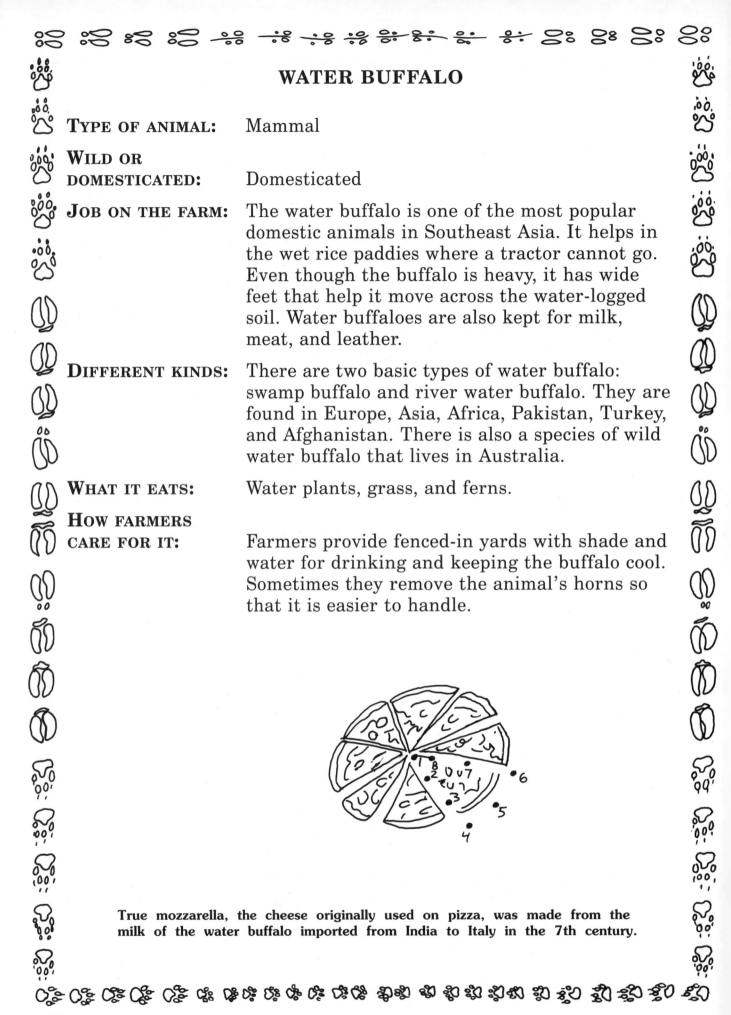

True mozzarella, the cheese originally used on pizza, was made from the milk of the water buffalo imported from India to Italy in the 7th century.

WOLF

TYPE OF ANIMAL:	Mammal
WILD OR DOMESTICATED:	Wild in most cases.
JOB ON THE FARM:	A wolf is not kept on a farm, but is a dangerous visitor. It may eat animals being kept there.
DIFFERENT KINDS:	There are about 15 different types; the most common is the gray wolf.
WHAT IT EATS:	Wolves will eat almost any animal they can catch. If hunting in a pack, they will even attack animals larger than they are.
HOW FARMERS CARE FOR IT:	Farmers can limit wolf visits by getting rid of dead animals, keeping births in or near farm buildings, and not housing young livestock in wooded pastures.

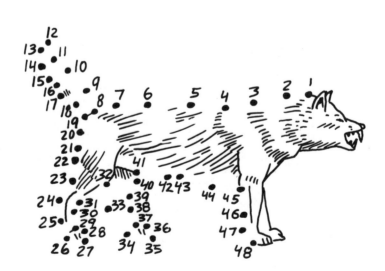

This is what a wolf probably looked like 37 million years ago.

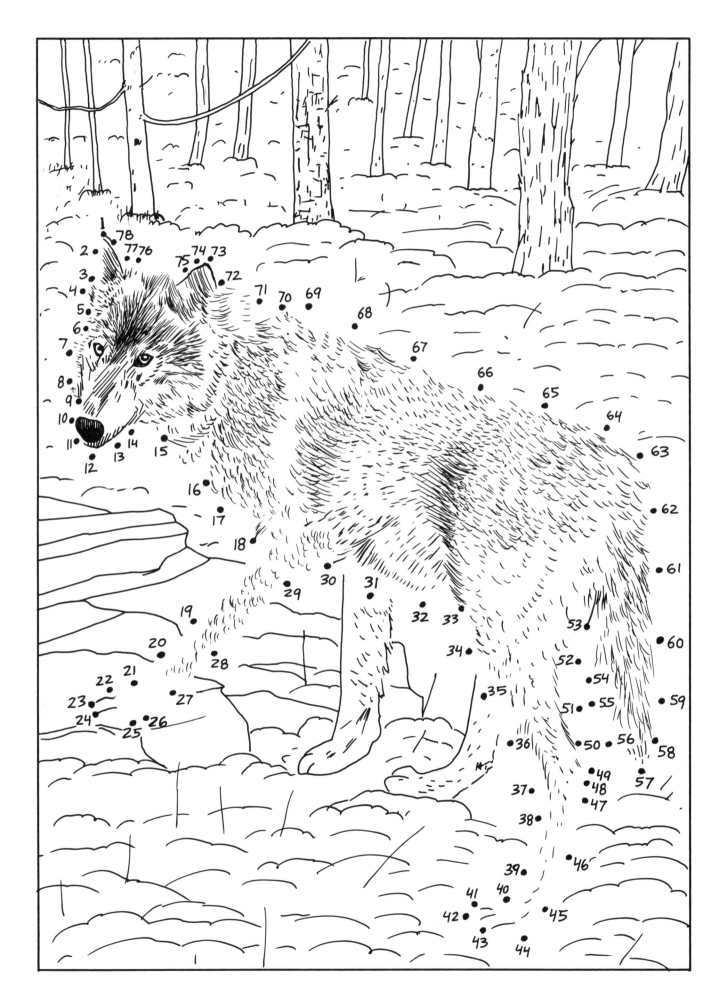

YAK

TYPE OF ANIMAL: Mammal

WILD OR DOMESTICATED: Domesticated

JOB ON THE FARM: There are about 12 million yaks in China. They are kept for their milk, their meat, their fur, and for work. Their job is carrying things; they might travel 12 to 18 miles (20 to 30km) a day with a load of 130 pounds (59kg) on steep paths.

DIFFERENT KINDS: There are three basic types of yak—Valley, Plateau Grassland, and the White Yak.

WHAT IT EATS: Yaks graze on grass in the summer and on shrubs in deep snow in the winter.

HOW FARMERS CARE FOR IT: The yak needs less care than cattle. It doesn't necessarily need shelter because of its plentiful fur, and it feeds by grazing. Land for grazing, water, and shade in the summer are needed.

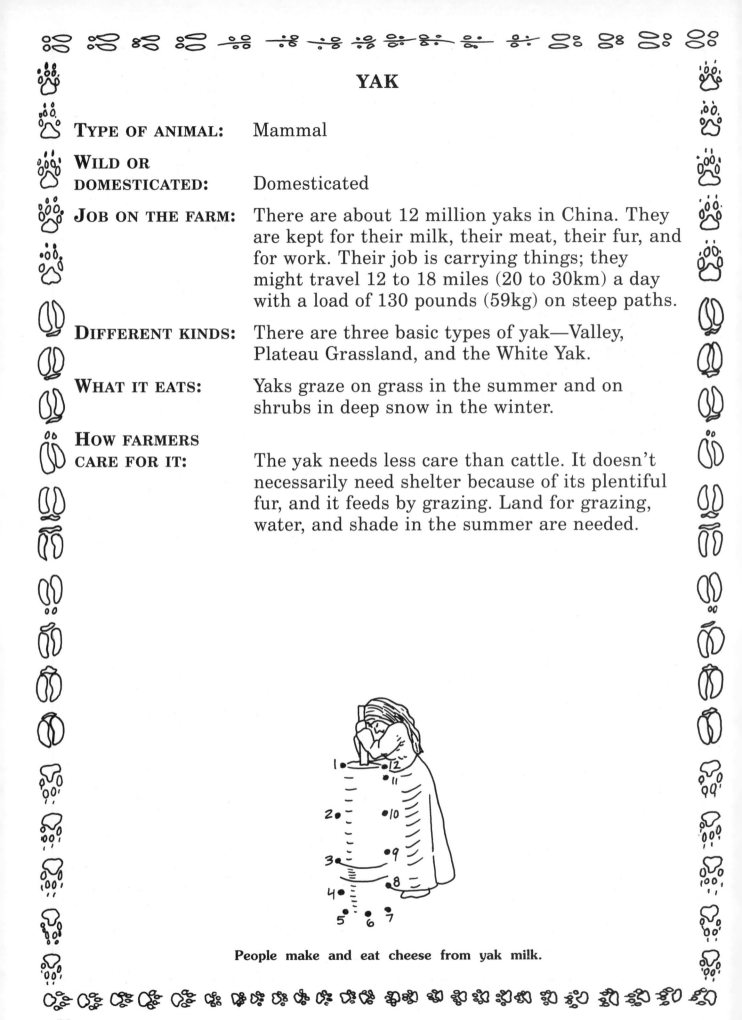

People make and eat cheese from yak milk.

INDEX